Midlands Buses
1950~1969

MIDLAND
COVENTRY
VIA ASH GREEN
747
11
GOLD L
NHA 782
STANDERWICK BLACKPOOL
NFR 956

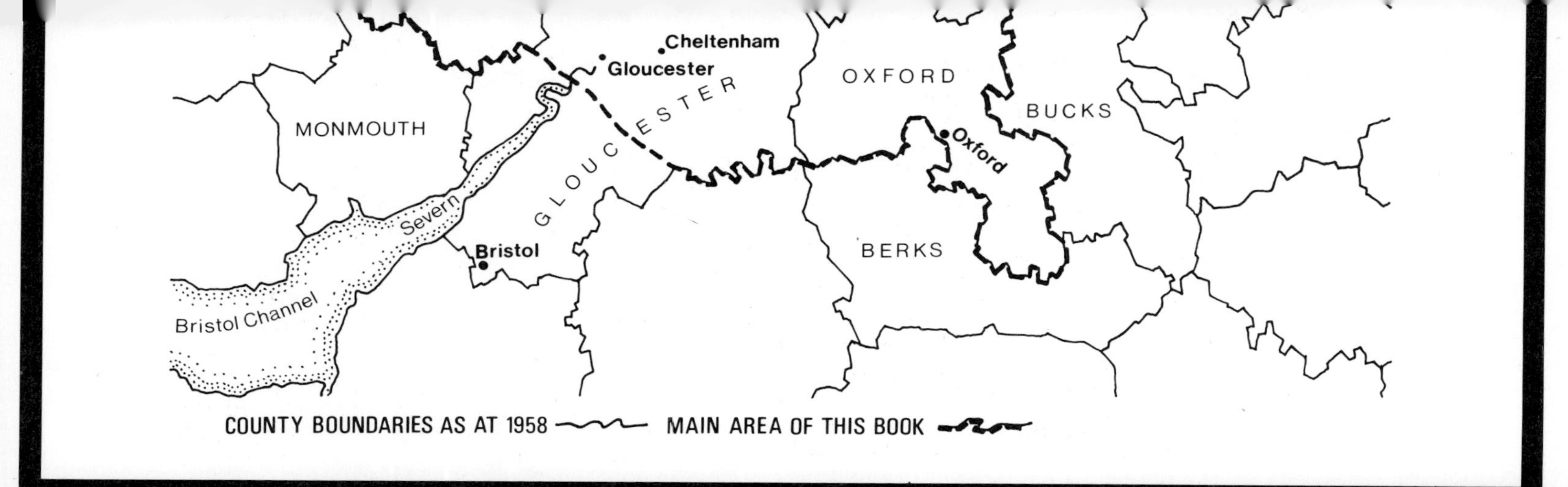

Birmingham — Birmingham City Transport; Birmingham & Midland Motor Omnibus Co (at Smethick)

Burton-upon-Trent — Burton Corporation Transport. Stevenson's (at Spath, Uttoxeter)

Cannock — Churchbridge Luxury Coaches

Cheltenham — Cheltenham District Traction Co; Black & White Motorways

Chesterfield — Chesterfield Corporation Transport; East Midland Motor Services

Child's Ercall, Market Drayton — H. Butter & Co

Coventry — Coventry Corporation Transport

Derby — Derby Corporation Transport; Trent Motor Traction; Tailby & George (at Willington)

Gloucester — Red & White Motor Services garage (at Coleford)

Leicester — Leicester City Transport; Brown's Blue (at Markfield)

Ludlow — Corvedale Motors

Mansfield — Mansfield District Traction Co

Newark — W. Gash & Sons, Lincolnshire Road Car Co garage

Northampton — Northampton Corporation Transport; United Counties Omnibus Co

Nottingham — Nottingham City Transport; Barton Transport (at Chilwell); Midland General and Notts & Derby (at Langley Mill); West Bridgford UDC (at West Bridgford); South Notts (at Gotham)

Nuneaton — J. Lloyd & Son

Oxford — City of Oxford Motor Services; South Midland Motor Services

Stafford — Austin's of Stafford

Stoke-on-Trent — Potteries Motor Traction; F. Proctor & Son

Stratford-upon-Avon — Stratford-upon-Avon Blue Motors

Walsall — Walsall Corporation Transport; Harper Brothers (at Heath Hayes); Green Bus Co (at Rugeley)

West Bromwich — West Bromwich Corporation Transport

Whitchurch — Salopia Saloon Coaches

Wolverhampton — Wolverhampton Corporation Transport

Midlands Buses
1950~1969
A. F. Porter

IA
LONDON
IAN ALLAN LTD

Contents

Cover:
Following the purchase of Dennis Loline I No 800 (600 DDH) Walsall acquired 16 Mark IIs. These were regularly used on route 6 to Sutton Coldfield and in this scene No. 882 (882 HDH), a Willowbrook-bodied vehicle new in 1960, stands at the Victoria Road terminus in Sutton Coldfield on 14 May 1961. *A. F. Porter*

First published 1985

ISBN 0 7110 1490 6

Published by Ian Allan Ltd, Shepperton, Surrey; and printed by Ian Allan Printing Ltd at their works at Coombelands in Runnymede, England

CINDERHILL
LONDON and MANCHESTER
HOME ALES ARE BEST
381C

Introduction

If it should be possible to identify a period of years which, more than any other, continuously sustained more than ordinary interest in public service vehicle development and operation, it is arguably the period covered by this album – the 1950s and 1960s. Personal preferences, or age, or background, might well identify another time for other individuals but few will argue, I suspect, with the suggestion that the 1950s and much of the decade that followed were years packed with interest for those who played a part in, or merely watched, the development of public transport on our roads. For some, no doubt – and the case has been well argued – the 1930s held a greater interest; they were pioneering years, still, but during the decade solid work was done and both technology and operational techniques carried road passenger transport forward in a highly recognisable form and one, indeed, that was to represent the norm for another 20 years. But for me, and for very many more, there can be no argument; the 1950s and the 1960s outshone all that went before and all that was to follow.

The 1950s gave us the first glimpse of new PSV technology that was, with some further innovation, to dominate the next quarter-century and indeed still, today, to be accepted normality. For much of the same decade, however, there had been stability, the perpetuation of the soundest, long-established, principles, and roads on which, as we might nowadays observe, 'a bus looked like a bus'. We had still, too, the pleasure of the company of prewar veterans in large numbers, some modernised but many quite unchanged, all fulfilling – or usually so – the expectations of their builders and operators – and their passengers.

The 1960s saw consolidation. All innovation that had proved worthwhile was exploited to the full; technology, it seemed, was almost limitless. But patterns developed, the less-than-wholly successful found quick abandonment, and the new, most stable, norm emerged. By the end of the decade the image that is with us today had substantially replaced the bus that once had looked like one. It was a fascinating period to observe and record. Mine, for much of the 1960s, was a somewhat distant view, followed assiduously through the pages of most publications available but, for all that, distant still. The exotic stood, for me, where once had been the everyday familiarity of Midlands roads and their never-ending stream of virtuously solid British marques. My cameras were aimed at anything that moved – right and proper, surely, for the all-round transport devotee – and much that was both quaint and curious came to be recorded under hot – and chilly – suns. But the fascination of the 1950s and the 1960s lingers on, almost as real today as when the last batch of prewar COG5s left Birmingham for the breaker's yard or, with luck, for some perceptive independent owner's fleet; as real as when BMMO put the splendid D9 into production, or sent CM5T coaches off down the M1 at unprecedented speeds; and as real as when Barton put the most extraordinary and enterprising fleet imaginable on the road.

If it is an acceptable premise that the 1950s and the 1960s were decades of quite exceptional interest in public transport matters, it seems equally acceptable to suppose that few areas of the British Isles could have provided a greater concentration of that interest than what might loosely be regarded as the 'Midlands'. Draw its perimeters, precisely or vaguely, where you will – my own choice being no less arbitrary than any other – and the 'Midlands' you so define were, in the period illustrated here, immensely rich and varied. That richness and variety spread from Megastar Midland Red doing its own thing on the grandest possible scale to the Sutton Coldfield Old People's Welfare Committee speeding its charges on voyages of delight in its once-proud London Transport 'Q', CGJ 188.

My chosen perimeters include all the obvious counties – Derbyshire, Nottinghamshire, Leicestershire, Northamptonshire, Oxfordshire,

Warwickshire, Worcestershire, Shropshire and Staffordshire – together with Gloucestershire, as far as Cheltenham and – an indulgence this to squeeze in a Red & White Motor Services Albion Valkyrie – Coleford. All the BET and BTC companies which had their bases within that arbitrary perimeter are represented, as are all the municipal fleets. More than a dozen independents appear – and only space, or lack of it, prevents a dozen more appearing. From beyond those perimeters come outsiders, BET's North Western, BTC's Bristol and Lincolnshire, the latter from the mystic east and full of promise, all on stage carriage services and, indeed, with an occasional interloping garage, in the finest traditions, representing the outposts of empire. Long-haul coaches dropped in with unnerving frequency, bringing wholly alien names to sober Midland streets. Ribble, Yorkshire Woollen District and, God help us, Northern General Transport, Geordie-packed. It was a fascinating time, when some romance still attached to travel and the yawns of bored sophisticates had not yet removed the excitement of these most foreign liveries, some of which might well have come 300 miles or more, no CM5T performance to soften the rigours of the journey.

It was a fascinating time and it has been a fascinating task assembling what I hope is an acceptable pictorial representation of it.

Acknowledgements
The majority of the photographs in this album are my own, mostly concentrated in the years 1960 to 1962. The necessary balance of illustrations, more broadly covering the 1950s and 1960s, however, has been made possible by the help of the following people and organisations in providing photographs. The help of all of them is most gratefully acknowledged and is individually credited. They are: Geoffrey Atkins, John Cull, Robert Mack, Roy Marshall, Robert Mills, Tom Moore (also representing the late Alan Cooper), R. H. G. Simpson, Midland Red, and the West Midlands Passenger Transport Executive.

The historical background to the operators and their vehicles has been drawn from many sources, including very many of the Ian Allan publications of the period and some more recently published. Other publications which have been used as sources of reference are those of the Omnibus Society, The PSV Circle, the Transport Publishing Company, Oxford Publishing Company, David & Charles, Autobus Review Publications, Fleetline Books, the Light Railway Transport League (now the Light Rail Transit Association), Birmingham Transport Historical Group, Leicester City Transport and PMT. Without these sources the album would have been sadly deficient.

Direct help and information has been given by City of Oxford Motor Services, East Midland Motor Services, Midland Red, Potteries Motor Traction, Trent Motor Traction, Chesterfield Transport Department, Leicester City Transport, City of Nottingham Transport, West Midlands PTE, Barton Transport, the Black Country Museum, the Museum of British Road Transport, the Omnibus Society, by the following individuals: Geoffrey Atkins, John Bennett, John Cull, Philip Groves, Robert Mack, Roy Marshall, Alan Mills, Robert Mills, Tom Moore, Don Phipps, John Skidmore, and by staff at West Bromwich and Wolverhampton Central Libraries.

The help they gave in responding so willingly to my harassment has been very much appreciated and is gratefully acknowledged. For those I may have overlooked go my apologies. For my errors and my wrong assumptions I blame myself and hope they'll pass unnoticed.

A. F. Porter
Northumberland
1984

The Municipal Undertakings

Few complexities exist to necessitate anything but the simplest form of introduction to the local authority transport undertakings which are illustrated in this album. Every local authority which had a transport undertaking in the geographical area which has been described in the Introduction, quite arbitrarily, to be the 'Midlands' has been represented. Beyond that, there is little to say. Most points of interest concerning an undertaking generally, or vehicles or groups of vehicles in its fleet, are made in the captions themselves – not exhaustively, of course, but at least, it is hoped, to enable a balanced overall view of the 1950s and 1960s to be obtained.

The structure of local government which was in existence during the 1950s/1960s had been long established by 1950 and was to continue unchanged until 1974 when the complete reorganistion of local government took place, on which subject not a word will be uttered, beyond, perhaps, reminding anyone who might care to listen that the original Passenger Transport Authorities and their Passenger Transport Executives, including that in the West Midlands, were created under the provisions of the Transport Act, 1968, and not the Local Government Act, 1972, which created the new local authorities themselves.

Most local authority transport undertakings in existence in 1950 probably had their origins in a tramway undertaking authorised under the provisions of the Tramways Act, 1870, in local Acts, allowing them to operate omnibuses as well as tramcars, in ss. 101 to 104 of the Road Traffic Act, 1930, also authorising them, subject to the consent of the Area Traffic Commissioners, to acquire and run omnibuses where they were already operating a transport undertaking, or by the acquisition of private transport companies already operating in their areas. Trolleybus operation depended on local Acts. All 12 municipal undertakings represented here had their origins within this range of enabling powers and all but West Bridgford Urban District Council, which never operated or owned a tramway, had their operating origins in tramways. West Bromwich too was something of an exception in that it had owned the tracks but had no tramcars, depending on other operators for services within the town. All the tramways in the area covered by this book had closed entirely before 1 January 1950, with the exception of those operated by Birmingham City Transport. Birmingham's tramways had been substantially replaced by trolleybuses and motorbuses by then but the last tram did not run its final journey until July 1953. Ironically, the last trolleybuses had been withdrawn in 1951.

Birmingham City Transport was by far the largest municipal operator in the Midlands and its fleet was to form the bulk of the West Midlands Passenger Transport Executive fleet on its creation in 1969, when the former City Transport undertaking was joined by those of Walsall, West Bromwich, and Wolverhampton. Not only was it influential in terms of its sheer size, but also in the way its policies were accepted as sensible, practical, and sound. That influence is still apparent today, more than 15 years after the last Daimler Fleetline to be owned by Birmingham City Transport was placed in service.

Birmingham City Transport

Above:
Nos 387 and 474 (OG 387 and OV 4474) were 1930 and 1931
AEC Regents rebodied with Brush 51-seat utility bodies
during the war. Several of the type were withdrawn before
the war but almost all of those which received Brush bodies
survived until 1950. The photograph was taken in 1950
shortly after their withdrawal.   *Robert Mills*

Below:
No 292 (EOG 292) was one of 85 Leyland TD6cs with Metro-
Cammell 52-seat bodywork, the city's first major Leyland
purchase, placed in service in 1938/9. It was photographed at
Oxhill Road terminus in 1952.   *Robert Mills*

Left:

The mainstay of Birmingham's trolleybus fleet were Metro-Cammell bodied Leyland's introduced from 1934 to 1940, all of which survived until the end of the system in 1951. No 40 (OC 1140) was a TTBD2 with 58-seat body new in 1934. It was photographed at the city boundary, probably around 1950. *Robert Mack*

Below:

Birmingham's standardised fleets are not wholly a postwar phenomenon. Of almos t 1,000 buses placed in service between 1934 and 1939 all but some 150 were Daimler COG5s. Typical of the earlier batches was No 726 (AOP 726), new in 1935 and carrying Metro-Cammell bodywork seating 48. No 726 itself was withdrawn in 1947 but several double- and single-deck vehicles built in 1935 lasted until 1950 and 25 only a year or two younger survived until 1960. *West Midlands PTE*

Right:

RT-type AEC Regent III No 1636 (GOE 636) with Park Royal 54-seat body at Acocks Green on 30 March 1962. The 15 vehicles of this comparatively unusual type were, apart from the Bridgemaster demonstrator 3228 (9 JML), the only postwar AEC vehicles acquired by the undertaking until 18 AEC Swifts were placed in service in 1967. They were built in 1947 and were all withdrawn between 1962 and 1964, 1636 being one of the last two to be withdrawn. None has been preserved.
A. F. Porter

Right:
Crossley DD42/6 No 2335 (JOJ 335) with Crossley 54-seat body on Olton Boulevard East on 1 April 1962. After 10 similar all-Crossley vehicles, though with HOE7 engines, had been introduced in 1949 a further 260 all-Crossley vehicles, of which 2335 was one, were added to the fleet in 1949 and 1950, all with 7/4B or 7/5B engines. The final 100 of these had the 'Birmingham' grille used on several chassis types and finally used on the 125 Crossley-bodied Daimler CVGs built in 1953 and 1954. *A. F. Porter*

Left:
The solitary AEC Bridgemaster to be acquired by the undertaking was No 3228 (9 JML), placed in service as an AEC demonstrator in 1956 and acquired in the following year. It had a 72-seat Crossley body, but, although another AEC Bridgemaster demonstrator also ran in Birmingham from 1958 in City Transport livery, it was a type that found no favour. No 3228 was largely confined to the 14 group of routes to the Tile Cross Estate and is seen here on 1 April 1962 on the 14E short working to Lea Village, Kitts Green. it was withdrawn 1969.   *A. F. Porter*

Right:
Birmingham City Transport committed itself to the Daimler Fleetline in 1963 but did so only after the purchase of 10 Leyland Atlanteans in 1961 and 10 Fleetlines in 1962. An Atlantean PDR1 demonstrator was placed in service in the City Transport livery in 1960, without fleet number, but, like the other 10 PDR1s, was acquired in 1961 and allocated fleet No 3230. Identified only as 460 MTE this vehicle is in this picture operating the short route from Suffolk Street in the city centre to Ladywood on 15 April 1961, prior to purchase.   *A. F. Porter*

Below right:
Standardisation on the Daimler CRG6 Fleetline with Park Royal or, like the Atlanteans, Metro-Cammell, bodywork rapidly followed the initial purchase of small batches of both types and the delivery of Birmingham City Transport's final order for 100 Fleetlines with Park Royal bodywork did not begin until shortly after the operator was taken over by the West Midlands Passenger Transport Executive. In this picture Birmingham's first Fleetline, 3241 (241 DOC) is at Old Square, Queensway, on 29 September 1962. It carries Metro-Cammell 72-seat bodywork. By the time the PTE took over on 1 October 1969, 610 Fleetlines, beginning with 3241 in 1962, had been placed in service, whilst the 100 on order were still to come.   *A. F. Porter*

Below:
Although it carried Birmingham City Transport livery throughout the period of its demonstration in the city, the 1958 AEC Bridgemaster with 72-seat Park Royal bodywork, 2211 MK, was allocated no fleet number. Like No 3228 it worked the 14 group of routes. On 14 August 1960 it was working the main route to Tile Cross Estate and was photographed in the city centre.   *A. F. Porter*

95
LADYWOOD
M&B It's Marvellous Beer
CAFE
PLAYER'S
cigarettes
STRAND
460 MYE

43
NECHELLS
FROM CITY
GOLD LEAF
241 DOC

Above:

1967 saw the Corporation's departure from several years' standardisation on the Daimler Fleetline with the purchase of Ford R192s and AEC Swifts. Twelve Fords were bought, all with Strachan 46-seat front-entrance bodywork. No 3651 (JOL 651E), the first of the batch, was photographed when new in 1967, somewhere on the short but meandering outer suburban route between King's Heath and West Heath via Bournville and Northfield. *T. W. Moore*

Below:

After delivery of the Ford R192s and AEC Swifts – of which 18 were bought – in 1967 the corporation resumed the acquisition of Daimler Fleetlines. A noticeable departure from the very marked preference for the double-deck Fleetline had already occurred, however, in 1965 with the delivery of 24 single-deck versions of the CRG6, all with Marshall 37-seat front-entrance bodywork. No 3451 (BON 451C), yet another first of the batch, is seen in 1965 on another outer suburban route – introduced in 1963 – the very short route 4 from Cotteridge to Pool Farm. *T. W. Moore*

Burton-upon-Trent Corporation Transport

Above:

Although the Burton fleet was small it offered much of interest before it became East Staffordshire District Council's transport undertaking under local government reorganisation in 1974. Although a solitary Daimler CWA6 was delivered during the war it was not until 1962 that Burton made any significant departure from Guy buses, turning again to Daimler when the group acquired the interests of Guy Motors Ltd. The undertaking's Guy Arabs were, however, far from standardised. In this picture No 5 (FA 8598), a 1947 Arab III with Roberts 53-seat lowbridge bodywork, is travelling along High Street, Burton, on 11 September 1961.   *A. F. Porter*

Right:

The first double-deckers to be acquired by Burton, Guy Arab IIs with Weymann and Park Royal 56-seat utility bodies, appeared in 1944, further similar vehicles and the solitary Daimler, following in 1945. In 1953, it bought six former London Passenger Transport Board Guy Arab IIs with Park Royal 56-seat utility bodies. No 70 in the Burton fleet (HGC 130), formerly London Transport G351, crosses the Trent in Burton on 27 September 1962. This vehicle is now preserved as London Transport G351.   *A. F. Porter*

Right:
Whilst the Burton undertaking took advantage of second-hand purchases it did not depend on them for its survival and modestly enhanced its fleet with the purchase of new buses. In 1957 it acquird two Guy Arab IVs and between 1959 and 1961 placed a further six of the type, with Massey 61-seat bodies, in service. The metalwork on No 77 (NFA 877), the last but one of this batch, catches the sun and momentarily dazzles as it takes a corner near the town centre on 29 August 1962. *A. F. Porter*

Below:
Burton-upon-Trent, like Birmingham, placed single-deck Fleetlines in service, with three 33ft long Willowbrook-bodied 44-seat vehicles in 1969. No 104 (MFA 704G) was photographed on the road bridge over the River Trent on 7 July 1969. *T. W. Moore*

Chesterfield Corporation Transport

Below:

For postwar reconstruction Chesterfield turned to Leyland and Crossley, buying a small fleet of all-Crossley double-deckers and single-deckers in 1947 and 1948. SD42/7 No 15 (NRA 715), new in 1948, waits to leave for Hasland from near the town centre in the early 1950s. *Roy Marshall*

Bottom:

Chesterfield, never a large undertaking, succeeded in operating a very varied fleet of vehicles where many undertakings of a similar size chose the simplicity of standardisation – occasionally, as with Northampton for example, perpetuating a combination of chassis type and a single coachbuilder's bodywork for several years. Chesterfield, however, spurned that option and chose instead the more daring application of new techniques as they became available and the occasional imaginative purchase of vehicles suited to the undertaking's operational requirements when an opportunity arose. In 1963 London Transport withdrew its three AEC Reliances with Willowbrook 42-seat bodies after only three years in service. Chesterfield bought them, tending at the time to favour single-deck vehicles. Here No 20 (497 ALH), formerly London Transport RW3, is seen in Chesterfield in May 1964. *G. H. F. Atkins*

Coventry Corporation Transport

Left:
Though there were several departures from its basic preference the city's primary vehicle choice was Daimler, from before the war until the undertaking was acquired by the West Midlands Passenger Transport Executive in 1974. Sound maintenance allowed the use of some prewar vehicles which had survived the blitz more or less unscathed to continue into the mid-1950s. Prominent amongst those which did, luckily, so survive was 170 (BKV 170), a Daimler COA6 built in 1937 and still carrying its original, albeit substantially rebuilt, Brush 55-seat body. It is seen in this photograph in Trinity Street, Coventry, on 25 October 1952. *A. A. Cooper/T. W. Moore*

Below:
Amongst the less usual non-Daimler vehicles operated by Coventry were nine Maudslay Regent IIIs with 58-seat Metro-Cammell bodies. These entered service on 1 January 1951, reviving the undertaking's original preference for Maudslay chassis after an interval of nearly 20 years. These nine vehicles were, however, the last Maudslay Regents to be built, and they survived intact as a group until 1965. No 119 (JKV 119), the third of the batch, is on a lunchtime factory service in Manor Road, Coventry, in this 1959 springtime scene. *T. W. Moore*

Above:
Perhaps typifying the Coventry fleet as effectively as anything of the period prior to the rather belated introduction of Atlanteans and Fleetlines in 1964 and 1965 was the batch of 95 Daimler CVA6s placed in service between 1948 and 1950, all with Metro-Cammell 60-seat bodies. In this picture 28 (FHP 28), the last of a 1946 order for the type, passes 94, one of the last of the type to be placed in service, in Pool Meadow bus station on 25 June 1962. *A. F. Porter*

Below:
Quite untypical of the fleet, though with a 58-seat body very similar to those on the CVA6s, was the solitary Crossley DD42/7 built in 1951 with Metro-Cammell bodywork. This vehicle, No 100 (GKV 100), is seen at the bus station, also on 25 June 1962. Its livery was the reverse of that in normal use on double-deckers and was kept throughout its life. *A. F. Porter*

Above:
Relatively few single-deck buses were used by Coventry and most of those which were acquired, after the early preference for Maudslay vehicles, were Daimlers. Sixteen CVD6s were delivered by Daimler in 1949 in two batches, each with almost identical 34-seat Brush bodies. No 115 (HKV 115), was placed in service on 1 October 1949, numerically the penultimate member of the second batch but followed by 114 and 116 to complete the order. It, too, was photographed on 25 June 1962.   *A. F. Porter*

Right:
Three Daimler Freelines with Wilowbrook 41-seat coachwork were acquired by Coventry for private hire work in 1959. Some years later they were relegated to stage carriage work and 403 (XRW 403) is seen here on such a duty in Coventry in the mid-1960s.
T. W. Moore

Far right, top:
Coventry Corporation had the distinction in 1967 of being the first non-THC undertaking to buy Bristol vehicles following the relaxation of the restrictions on sales. The corporation's choice was the RESL6G with Eastern Coach Works bodies. No 516 (KHP 516E) was the first of six to be acquired — 516 to 518 having 44-seat front-entrance bodywork and 519 to 521 having 42-seat dual-doorway bodywork. It is seen on 30 January 1967. *T. W. Moore*

Derby Corporation Transport

Below:

Like many of the smaller municipal transport undertakings Derby provided interest that, perhaps, belied its size. Most postwar deliveries were on Daimler chassis, with an isolated departure from that preference in 1952, when five Foden PVD6s and five Crossley DD42/8As were acquired, all with Brush 56-seat bodies. The preponderance of Daimler motorbuses had its compensation, however, in the trolleybus system which, small though it was, had its third postwar extension opened in 1953 and eight new trolleybuses placed in service in 1960. The first conversion of a trolleybus route to motorbus operation took place, nevertheless, only two years later and the final abandonment came in 1967. Typical of the two main batches of Daimlers provided between 1947 and 1950 is No 36 (BCH 136), a CVD6 with a Brush – in this case 8ft wide – 56-seat body, photographed in Victoria Street, Derby, on 29 July 1960.   A. F. Porter

Above:

Two Sunbeams stand in the Market Place, Derby, on 27 September 1962. No 180 (RC 8880) was a W, with British Thomson-Houston electrical equipment, in a batch built from 1944 to 1946 and fitted with Park Royal 56-seat utility bodies. No 191 (ARC 491) was an F4 with BT-H equipment and a Brush 56-seat body, new in 1948. A Daimler CVG6 seems to be squeezing through a constricted space alongside 191. *A. F. Porter*

Left:

No 237 (SCH 237) was the second of the final batch of trolleybuses to enter service at Derby. It was a Sunbeam F4A with electrical equipment supplied by AEI and a Roe 65-seat body. It is at work here near the Chellaston terminus on 27 September 1962, and was subsequently privately preserved. *A. F. Porter*

Leicester City Transport

Above right:

Leicester's 25 AEC Renowns were the 30ft 664 version, built in 1939/40, several years after most others. No 334 (DBC 225) of this well-known fleet was built in 1940 and carried a 64-seat Metropolitan-Cammell body. It is seen here in the city centre, probably in 1948, and was withdrawn in 1958. *Roy Marshall*

Right:

Leicester acquired only two new vehicles during the war years, and by the end of 1945 some 60% of the city's services were still provided by its tramways. In 1946, however, 18 AEC Regent IIs and 20 Leyland Titan PD1s were placed in service. No 238 (DJF 339), an all-Leyland vehicle with 56-seat body, was photographed at the Melton Road terminus in September 1949. Several of this batch were sold to Barton Transport in 1949 and 1950 and this particular vehicle appears later as Barton's No 844. *Roy Marshall*

ENAMEL PAINT
HUMBERSTONE RD
DBC 225
334
LEICESTER CITY TRANSPORT

GOODWIN'S Extra Self-Raising FLOUR
DJF 339
238

Above:
Six 1946-built AEC Regal Is with Weymann 35-seat bodies were acquired from Devon General in 1952 in exchange for six of Leicester's 1946 Regent IIs. No 200 (HTT 504), formerly Devon General SR504, is seen on Leicester's Inner Circle, largely the preserve of these vehicles. It was withdrawn in 1963. *Roy Marshall*

Below:
Between 1948 and 1950 160 new buses were placed in service to replace the remaining tramcars and most of the surviving prewar buses. No 9 (FBC 275), an AEC Regent III with Metro-Cammell 56-seat body was one of the first of that replacement fleet and was new in 1948. Its seating capacity was increased to 60 in 1957. *Roy Marshall*

Above:

Although the undertaking had, albeit somewhat tentatively, placed three Atlanteans in service in 1963 front-engined double-deckers were still being delivered until January 1968, when the last Leyland PD3A/12 was delivered. Much of the tram replacement fleet of 1948 to 1950 was to remain in service, indeed, until the arrival of the first main batch of the rear-engined fleet, 20 Atlanteans, between December 1968 and April 1969. Two of the 1949/50 delivery of all-Leyland PD2/1s which so survived were 143 (FJF 182) and 129 (FJF 168), seen here in new and original liveries in Charles Street in 1965.   *T. W. Moore*

Below:

Coventry's lead in the purchase of Bristol buses was followed later in 1967 by Leicester, which bought its first Bristols in the autumn of that year. No 1 in the city fleet (LJF 1F) was an RESL6L with Eastern Coach Works 42-seat dual-doorway bodywork. It was photographed on 3 November 1967, in Charles Street, Leicester, soon after entering service.   *T. W. Moore*

Northampton Corporation Transport

Below:
One of the last survivors of Northampton's prewar fleet was 103 (VV 7875), a Daimler COG5 with, typically, Roe bodywork – in this case seating 55. 103 was built in 1939 and survived until the early 1960s. It was photographed in Northampton, probably in the early 1950s.   *R. F. Mack*

Bottom:
The Northampton philosophy for very many years seems to have been that it is better to adhere to what has been tried and tested than to rush into unnecessary experimentation with unproven techniques, newfangled concepts, and the products of unfamiliar manufacturers. It smacks, of course, of cautious conservatism and it is, too, perhaps indicative of something to do with the love of precedent that is so often found in local government. For all that near-criticism, however, the undertaking was sustained for more than 30 years by almost nothing but the most orthodox rear entrance, open platform, vehicles. From 1937 to 1968 the undertaking bought one Leyland and 10 Crossleys; its other purchases were all Daimlers, most frequently carrying Roe bodywork. To give a single picture that typifies the fleet as it was for so long presents no problems. Daimler CVG6 179 (ANH 179), one of a batch built in 1949/50 with Roe 56-seat bodies, stops to pick up at Castle Station on 20 July 1962.   *A. F. Porter*

Nottingham City Transport

Above:
A solitary 1937 AEC Regal, 779 (DAU 454), was converted to mobile canteen use in 1959 and lasted in this form – as No 801 – for a few years. Apart from 801 the last prewar vehicles in the city's fleet were withdrawn from service in 1959. They were AEC Regents, one of which, No 10 (ETO 494), with English Electric bodywork, is seen here, probably in the late 1940s.   *Roy Marshall*

Right:
Like many operators Nottingham had its wartime utility buses, an enforced departure from its preference for AEC products. Daimler CWA6 61 (GTV 761), carrying Northern Counties 56-seat bodywork, stands at Trent Boulevard terminus in August, 1950. No 61 was still in service nine years later, the year of its withdrawal, the last survivor of the type in Nottingham's fleet.   *G. H. F. Atkins*

Left:

The clear preference for AEC products lasted until 1965 when, although many Leyland PD2s, Atlanteans, and Daimler Fleetlines were in service, or on order, 35 AEC Renowns were bought. The largest postwar acquisition of AEC vehicles, however, was in 1953/54, when 72 AEC Regent IIIs with 56-seat Park Royal bodywork were obtained. One of that batch, No 151 (OTV 151), goes round the City Square to a background of the Griffin and Spalding emporia on 31 July 1960. *A. F. Porter*

Below:

Unlike its near-neighbour Derby the Nottingham undertaking bought no new trolleybuses for its extensive electric traction system after 1952, but the system lasted almost as long as Derby's, closing the final route – which had been its first – on 30 June 1966. In the 1930s, indeed, trolleybuses outnumbered motorbuses in the fleet but by 1960 fewer than 200 trolleybuses remained whilst the motorbus fleet had grown to more than 300 vehicles. Although the bulk of the trolleybus fleet that survived until closure had been built between 1948 and 1952 a few wartime vehicles held on almost to the end. No 464 (GTV 664) waits at Wells Road with 481 (KTV 481) on 2 April 1961. No 464 was one of a batch built in 1945/46 with Roe, Brush, or Park Royal 56-seat bodies on Karrier W chassis with BTH 207 electrical equipment. No 464's body was by Roe. No 481 was a Karrier F4 with BTH 209 equipment and a Roe 56-seat body, scarcely less austere than that on 464, new in 1948. *A. F. Porter*

Right:

Looming large, Nottingham's penultimate trolleybus, about to be passed by Regent 254, stands in City Square on 31 July 1960. No 600 (KTV 600) was a BUT 9641T with Metro-Vick 210 equipment built in 1952. A Brush 70-seat body was carried. No 254 (XTO 254) was an AEC Regent V with Park Royal 62-seat body built in 1956. *A. F. Porter*

Below right:

The last batch of the AEC-preference era to enter service with the City undertaking was that of 35 AEC Renowns built in 1965. These all had Park Royal 70-seat full-height bodywork. No 381 (DAU 381C), one of the last of the batch, was photographed nearing the city centre on a busy Saturday afternoon in September 1968. *T. W. Moore*

XTO 254
254
People love PLAYER
Gordon's
1·6
"TARANTELLA" PEELED TOMATOES
46 TRENT BRIDGE VIA ARKWRIGHT ST.
KTV 600

CAVENDISH
Telefusion FUSION
4 1 CINDERHILL
ASSORTED
LONDON and MANCHESTER
HOME ALES BEST
DAU 381C

NGHAM REFRIGERATION LTD
61 CLIFTON
PTO 712G

It's HIGHGATE for me!
MILD ALE
QUALITY & STRENGTH
REMOVALS
STORE
38
ASTON
401
YDH401

Left:
The arrival of non-AEC products in the Nottingham fleet in the 1960s did not spell the end of new AEC vehicles as a batch of Swifts arrived in 1969. AEC Swift No 712 (PTO 712G), bodied by Northern Counties, is seen in Canal Street, Nottingham, in August 1969.   *G. H. F. Atkins*

Walsall Corporation Transport

Below left:
An album of this size could be devoted entirely to this undertaking and its vehicles. In 1961 Walsall had a fleet that represented 27 different combinations of chassis and body manufacturers – not chassis types and body designs in different combinations, just their manufacturers. By 1965, that combination stood at 21 with a fleet of around 270 vehicles, including trolleybuses. Whilst the magnificently maintained but highly standardised Birmingham fleet was always a delight to see, the in-house products of Midland Red unparalleled, and the richness of the Midlands operators overall so splendid, there was nothing quite like Walsall and its fleet to be found outside the County Borough – or the far-flung places to which its routes had penetrated. Walsall's flavour was all its own. But that flavour, that diversity, represented not uncertainty and lack of conscious direction; quite the reverse. The undertaking was innovative, inventive, imaginative, and, without a doubt, under Mr Edgley Cox's leadership, a pioneer in public passenger transport. It was Edgley Cox's inspiration that produced for Walsall a trolleybus system worth far more than a second glance but it was that same foresight that broke the three-axle stranglehold that had long been imposed by the Ministry of Transport and freed all operators from the constraint. This was achieved with a 1954-built batch of 30ft Sunbeam F4A trolleybuses on two axles. A very different kind of initiative is shown, however, by this photograph of 401 (YDH 401) taken in Bradford Place, Walsall, on 15 April 1961. 401 was a Daimler CLG5 built in 1956. The 59-seat body was built in the undertaking's own workshops from components supplied by Metal Sections Ltd.   *A. F. Porter*

Top right:
No 800's claim to fame is that it was a Dennis Loline Mark I YFI and had been the 1958 show model. Walsall liked it and bought it, then bought another 16 Mark IIs. No 800 (600 DDH) had a Willowbrook 70-seat body and is seen here parked off St Paul's Street, Walsall, on 27 June 1961.   *A. F. Porter*

Right:
When this photograph was taken on 11 May 1961, the Walsall trolleybus system was still undergoing extension and vehicles were still being acquired, by their judicious purchase second-hand. No 302 (FTG 698) had in fact been obtained from the Pontypridd undertaking in 1956 and was by 1961 in use only at peak hours. It was a 1945 Karrier W and had a Roe 56-seat utility body.   *A. F. Porter*

Left:

Second-hand vehicles usually receive little more than new paintwork and a new identity. No 873 (HBE 542) was one such, like 302, to receive cosmetic treatment when it arrived in Walsall from Grimsby-Cleethorpes in 1960 after ten years of Lincolnshire coast service. Three other trolleybuses acquired from Grimsby-Cleethorpes at the same time underwent dramatic transformation in Walsall's own workshops, emerging two years or so after their acquisition lengthened to 30ft. Walsall similarly enhanced a few of its existing vehicles during the same period. The unaltered 873, seen here in St Paul's Street, Walsall, on 15 June 1961, was a Crossley Empire TDD43/2 with Metro-Vick electrical equipment. It had been built in 1951 with a Roe 54-seat body, which it still carried. *A. F. Porter*

Below:

Although three-axle buses were to reappear, and Huddersfield ordered three-axle trolleybuses as late as 1959, five years after Walsall cracked the Ministry's requirements for 30ft trolleybuses and three years after the requirement had been totally lifted, it was the Walsall experiment with 30ft two-axle Sunbeam F4A trolleybuses that ushered in the new standards. Walsall placed 22 of these handsome vehicles in service between 1954 and 1956. They had British Thomson-Houston electrical equipment and Willowbrook 70-seat bodies. No 854 (TDH 904) has just set down passengers in Walsall in this summer scene, probably in 1961. *A. F. Porter*

Right:
Much history lay beneath the prosaic destination 'Wolverhampton' on No 306 (BDY 812) as it stood in Wolverhampton Street, Walsall, on 12 May 1961 on the joint trolleybus service between the two towns. No 306 was a Sunbeam W4, built in Wolverhampton in 1947. It had British Thomson-Houston electrical equipment and a Weymann 56-seat body. When new, 306 had been supplied to the Hastings Tramways Company, a subsidiary of Maidstone & District Motor Services Ltd. The Hastings company was wholly absorbed by M&D in 1957 and in 1959 the trolleybus system was abandoned, the Sunbeam W4s being bought by the Maidstone, Bradford, and Walsall municipal undertakings. Walsall's final opportunity purchases were eight Sunbeam F4s acquired from the Ipswich undertaking in 1962/ 63.
A. F. Porter

Below:
The last former Walsall Corporation vehicles to remain in service with the West Midlands PTE — seeing more than a decade of PTE ownership — were a dozen or so of the last batch of short-length Daimler Fleetline CRG6LXs to be acquired by the corporation. No 119 (XDH 519G) — which became No 119L in the PTE fleet — was built in 1969 and carried Northern Counties 68-seat dual-doorway bodywork. It was photographed loading in Walsall in March 1970, five months after entering PTE service but still in Walsall's old livery. *T. W. Moore*

Above:
Evidence of Walsall's liking for Dennis chassis remained for several years after the last prewar Dennis had been withdrawn from passenger use and lasted well into the Dennis Loline era. Some saw use for driver training, or as snowploughs, and one became a mobile canteen. A very familiar vehicle that was parked through the railings at Birchills Depot for some years was Dennis 'E' No 54 (DH 5505), which had been built in 1926 and was rebodied by W. D. Smith of West Bromwich around 1935. It was withdrawn in 1950, used for some time as a towing vehicle, spent its retirement in the railings, and was sold for scrap in 1963. The photograph was taken on 4 August 1962.   *A. F. Porter*

Right:
One of the 1938 Dennis Lances (despite the 'Lancet' lettering) used for snowplough duties after withdrawal from passenger use in 1951 was No 193 (FDH 854). Still carrying its Park Royal body, though topless, No 193 was parked out of harm's way in Birchills Depot on 23 April 1961. Lance snowplough No 213 (FDH 874) can just be seen beyond it. No 213 ended its ploughing days that year but 193 survived for two years more.   *A. F. Porter*

West Bridgford Urban District Council

Above:

The smallest of the municipal operators in the Midlands in the 1950s and 1960s was at West Bridgford, an Urban District adjoining the southern outskirts of Nottingham. Powers had been obtained for its own transport service, independent of Nottingham, in 1912 and the first five buses, Dennis double-deckers, entered service in 1914. Although the fleet grew larger than this it was always small and in 1968 was acquired by Nottingham. No 23 (KAL 687) stands with two other West Bridgford buses at Trent Boulevard in June 1956. No 23 was an AEC Regent III built in 1948. It had a Park Royal 60-seat body. *G. H. F. Atkins*

Right:

Like adjoining Nottingham West Bridgford was an AEC Renown user. Nos 41 and 42 (BRR 241/2C) were East Lancashire-bodied 75-seat vehicles new in 1965 and were the first 30ft buses in the fleet. No 42 was caught by the camera when still only a few months old in Broad Marsh, Nottingham, in August 1965. *G. H. F. Atkins*

Bottom right:

West Bridgford joined the purchasers of the AEC Swift in 1967 with an order for three. No 43 (NAL 543F) was the first and carried East Lancs 45-seat bodywork. It was photographed in 1968 prior to the absorption of the undertaking by Nottingham. *T. W. Moore*

West Bromwich Corporation Transport

Above:

Sound and solid and rather unremarkable. This is not damnation by faint praise but it is difficult when the adjoining operators are Birmingham, Walsall, and Wolverhampton, and Midland Red, with all of which West Bromwich operated joint services, to see especial merit in merely sound and solid virtues. It was always a pleasure to see the undertaking's attractive livery – two shades of blue and much cream – coming up the long drag past Snow Hill Station into Colmore Row, Birmingham, or brightening the leafy lanes in Sutton Coldfield, but beyond the general attractiveness of the largely Daimler fleet – and, of course, the survival of the very well known Dennis 'E' No 32 (EA 4181) – it is not easy to say much more than 'nice try – pity about the neighbours'. It did, however, have four Dennis Lancet IIs new in 1937/38 with Jensen bodies, a combination not frequently found. 68 (EA 9062) was photographed at home base, probably in the early 1950s.   *Roy Marshall*

Below left:

Like No 116 (BEA 716) Daimler CWA6 126 (BEA 736) was one of a few wartime vehicles to receive new 56-seat Alexander bodies in 1953. The undertaking's attractive livery enhances even the lines of the austere Duple utility bodywork, seen here before 126 received its 1953 body.   *Roy Marshall*

Above:

Whilst several of the wartime Daimlers received new bodies in 1953 a few prewar vehicles lasted intact until the early 1960s. This was not unusual – it happened too with Midland Red, Birmingham, and a few other Midlands operators – though it was infrequent and only a very small proportion of vehicles in existence with major operators after 1959 were of prewar origin. The survivor shown in this illustration was, however, a little out of the ordinary. Daimler COG5 106 (BEA 36), built in 1940 and essentially a prewar vehicle, carried a Jensen 38-seat body. It was photographed in Rydding Road, Wednesbury, on 27 May 1960.   *A. F. Porter*

Below:

Amongst those wartime vehicles which received new bodies in 1953 was No 116 (BEA 716), a Daimler product of 1944. The new 56-seat body was by Alexander. No 116 is seen in action in Moor Street, West Bromwich, on 31 August 1961.   *A. F. Porter*

Left:
The Daimler CVG6 was an orthodox rear-entrance vehicle which remained popular with many operators for several years after high capacity rear-engine models had become readily available. The first encroachment of the new orthodoxy, rear engines with everything, did not, in fact, take place at West Bromwich until 1967, when the undertaking's first Daimler Fleetlines were bought. Until then the CVG6 met most of West Bromwich's demands. No 235 (735 FEA), shown here in Birmingham Road on the short climb out of Sutton Coldfield on 16 June 1962, was a CVG6-30 built in 1962 with Metro-Cammell 74-seat bodywork. *A. F. Porter*

Above:
No 108 (KEA 108E) was one of a batch of low-height Daimler Fleetline CRG6LXs with Metro-Cammell 73-seat bodywork placed in servic e in 1967. They were, with later Eastern Coach Works-bodied Fleetlines, to be the last former West Bromwich Corporation vehicles to remain in West Midlands PTE service, then numbered 101H to 121H. The first 13 of the batch – 102 to 114 (KEA 102-114E) – were the first Fleetlines in the West Bromwich fleet, whilst the original vehicle in the batch, No 101, was destroyed in a fire at Metro-Cammell prior to delivery. No 108 is seen en route to Wednesbury passing under a fairly conspicuously marked low bridge in Hyde Road, Wednesbury, on 23 May 1967, when new. *T. W. Moore*

Right:
The well-known Dixon-bodied 1929 Dennis 'E' No 32 (EA 4181) was set aside for preservation at a time when considerations of second-hand or scrap value, or at the very least of removing the clutter of unwanted obsolescence, were the epitomy of normality. The saving of No 32 was, by the standards of those times, almost as much an act of lunacy as an act of faith. It was, however, done. Some years later No 32 graces the precincts at another pioneering event, a British Railways Open Day at Tyseley Shed in Birmingham. There have been some changes made since this close-up of 32's radiator was taken on 29 September 1969. *A. F. Porter*

Wolverhampton Corporation Transport

Above:
The susceptibility of any local authority service to 'political' direction and, now and again, 'political' interference, is fairly well recognised, if only outside council chambers. Occasionally that direction, or that interference, reflects a genuine political philosophy. More often, probably, it reflects no more than individual whim coupled with a forceful personality or a loud voice, or perhaps, a not wholly incomprehensible wish on the part of councillors and their officers to be seen as people in the very forefront of progress and enlightenment; outsiders might, alternatively, see them as slaves of fashion. Transport, with most other services, has felt this influence. No self-respecting municipal undertaking allowed an electric tramway to pollute its streets with archaic rattling clanging tramcars, the antithesis of traffic-flow and sensible passenger transport movement ideology, for any longer after 1950 than it was absolutely obliged to. Patterns had been set and precedents – often enough with persuasive economic reasons that were valid enough locally and in the short term – established. But fashion and the aspirations of those who were the custodians of civic pride played their part. No authority that after 1950 invested in its tramways could any longer be seen, it seemed, to be in any way 'progressive'.

Wolverhampton, like most towns, probably, suffered from the whims of civic dignitaries – surface contact tramways, whilst all around were overhead – but whims can on occasion benefit, or show farsightedness. Wolverhampton ran motorbuses as long ago as 1905, displaying not a little flair. They were abandoned, in due course, but only for two years or so. From 1911 onwards their presence in the municipal undertaking's stock of vehicles has been uninterrupted.

Vehicle development in the undertaking was to a marked extent influenced by the presence of both the Guy and Sunbeam factories in the town and with the availability of locally made vehicles it is, perhaps, hardly surprising that Wolverhampton should have operated an extensive trolleybus system. It was, in fact, second only to Birmingham in the introduction of trolleybuses in the Midlands, placing the first new vehicles in service in 1923 as tram replacements, and completed the conversion of its tramways to trolleybus operation in 1930. Birmingham's tramway conversion was begun in 1922 but the limited trolleybus system was converted to motorbus operation in 1951, outlived by some major tram routes which the trolleybuses had originally been intended to replace, Wolverhampton, in marked contrast, did not abandon trolleybus operation until 1967, 44 years after its introduction.

In this picture, taken in Wednesfield Road, Wolverhampton, on 28 August 1961, Sunbeam W No 452 (EJW 452) is, appropriately, bound for Wednesfield. No 452 was one of two batches of Ws with British Thomson-Houston electrical equipment built from 1945 to 1947 which were rebodied by Roe from 1958 to 1961. The seating capacity was increased to 60 in the process.   *A. F. Porter*

Above:
Postwar developments in the undertaking were also to a marked extent influenced by Guy and Sunbeam – acquired by Guy in 1948 – continuing to offer locally built products. Few vehicles of any other make were placed in service. Looking rather more 'modern' than later Guy Arabs in service with the fleet this Arab IV, No 51 (4051 JW), one of a batch of 50 built from 1959 to 1961 and fitted with Metro-Cammell 72-seat bodies, waits in Cannock bus station on 4 August 1962, to return to Wolverhampton. Whilst the remainder of the batch were fitted with Gardner 6LW engines No 51 had a Meadows 6DC.   *A. F. Porter*

Below:
Sunbeam F4 No 615 (FJW 615), one of a batch with British Thomson-Houston electrical equipment and Park Royal 54-seat bodywork built in 1949/50, stands in Pinfold Street, Darlaston, on 22 March 1960. Darlaston was, at the time, an independent Urban District and one of several local authorities which were served by Wolverhampton Corporation Transport.   *A. F. Porter*

Above:
Guy Motors' most radical departure from the manufacture of traditional motorbuses came in 1959 with the introduction of the Wulfrunian, designed as a front-entrance vehicle with front engine and with many other innovative features. It had been designed largely to meet the requirements of the West Riding Automobile Company, a major independent operator at the time, and by whom most Wulfrunians were ultimately to be bought. It is, even so, hardly surprising that Wolverhampton Corporation should have toyed with this vehicle. It did so, to the extent of acquiring two, 70 (4070 JW) and 71 (4071 JW), built in 1961 and 1962 respectively with East Lancashire 72 and 71- seat bodies. They both led somewhat chequered careers with the undertaking, spending some periods out of use, but No 71 was fairly reliable and remained with the undertaking until 1973, the last of the type to remain in service with its first owner. No 70, pictured here in, probably, the mid-1960s, was the more 'conventional' of the two; 71 was unusual for the type in having a front grille rather than the normal louvred front panel, forward- rather than front-entrance body, and unique in having drum rather than disc brakes. *Roy Marshall*

Left:
From time to time Wolverhampton found itself turning to Birmingham City Transport for vehicles. Birmingham No 1587 (GOE 587), a 1947 Daimler CVG6 with Metro-Cammell 54-seat bodywork, was one of a batch hired from the City's undertaking in 1961 when part of the Wolverhampton trolleybus system was temporarily closed for roadworks. It is seen in this view on route 35 in Oxbarn Avenue on 6 March 1961. *A. F. Porter*

Above:
Although other operators acquired Fords in some numbers Wolverhampton – apart from three minibuses – placed only one in service, No 720 (KUK 720D), a Type R226 with Strachan 52-seat bodywork. No 720 was new in 1966 and is seen here in service on 30 July 1967.   *A. A. Cooper/T. W. Moore*

Below:
Even though only three years had passed between the delivery of AEC Reliances Nos 705 to 707 in the Wolverhampton fleet in 1963 and No 720 in 1966, it was to be another year before the missing 708 to 719 materialised. Nos 703-713 were Strachan-bodied AEC Swifts and 714-719 (NJW 714E to NJW 719E) were Daimler Roadliners with similar 53-seat bodywork. No 718 (NJW 718E), new in 1967, was photographed in West Midlands PTE ownership in April 1970 in Wolverhampton and still, but for the change in the legal owner's name, in Wolverhampton Corporation livery.   *T. W. Moore*

The British Electric Traction Group of Companies

For most of the period covered by this book and, indeed, until the National Bus Co and the first four Passenger Transport Authorities and their respective Passenger Transport Executives were established in 1969 bus operators in England and Wales fell into four categories – the municipal undertakings, the BET group, the British Transport Commission group (succeeded by the Transport Holding Co in 1962 when the Transport Commission was disbanded), and the independents, which were not controlled by any of the other groups. With the exception of a very few large independent operators, like Barton Transport, Lancashire United Transport and the West Riding Automobile Co, every major company operator, despite any external sign of its seeming autonomy, was controlled by either British Electric Traction or the British Transport Commission/ Transport Holding Co. Within the apparent simplicity of this categorisation there were, however, hidden complexities and some peculiarly complex company histories.

The BET group, whose constituent companies in the area covered by the album were the Birmingham & Midland Motor Omnibus Co, East Midland Motor Services, City of Oxford Motor Services, Potteries Motor Traction, the BMMO subsidiary, Stratford-upon-Avon Blue Motors, and Trent Motor Traction, had its origins in tramway operations and several of the constituent companies, though by no means all of them, had themselves begun as tramway operators. It was, however, an organisational structure within which the individual constituent companies operated the public transport services. The British Electric Traction Co Ltd controlled the constituent companies but did not itself provide transport services. Like many conglomerates, whilst it had its roots in a specific trading activity – in this case tramways – it expanded to the point at which, by the

time the member bus companies became constituents of the National Bus Co in 1969, it had controlling interests in trading concerns whose activities were often far removed from public transport and far removed from the British Isles. Diversification became the key to survival and the group, shorn of its home transport interests, survived and prospered. BET had been founded in 1895 with the object of developing electric tramways and immediately set about the task of acquiring a financial interest in as many non-electric tramway companies as it could obtain; many were electrified under BET control and some new companies were promoted. In association with its tramway objectives BET added several electricity supply companies to its holdings and tramway companies overseas. With the development of the motorbus BET's interests embraced transport concerns that had never operated tramways and under its control all its tramway operating companies were eventually to abandon electric traction in favour of the motor omnibus. The last constituent company to operate tramcars, the Gateshead & District Tramways Co, abandoned them in favour of motorbuses in 1951. All the BET group companies in the Midlands had converted their tramway operations to motorbuses, or had been acquired by a municipality, long before the period covered by this album begins.

The progenitor of the BET group with whose bus companies this album is concerned may have been the British Electric Traction Co but that company was not alone in controlling passenger transport companies in the period that generally can be taken as ending with the creation of the British Transport Commission in 1948 under the provisions of the Transport Act, 1947, and the polarisation of the major operating companies into the two groups. Before 1948 there had been the municipal undertakings, the independents, and three principal groups of operating companies – the British Electric Traction Co, the Tilling Group and Balfour Beatty. Like BET, both Tilling and Balfour Beatty had had tramway interests. Some 23 of the operating companies which were to fall into the BET and BTC groups in 1948 had from 1928 to 1942, however, been part of a hybrid gathering known as the Tilling & British Automobile Traction group, within which the group chairmanship was vested in alternate years in the Tilling Group and BET. Upon the dissolution of the hybrid the constituent companies went into the direct control of either Tilling Motor Services Ltd or BET Omnibus Services Ltd, though five of them were to pass from the control of one group to the control of the other before 1948.

Balfour Beatty's interests had been in electricity undertakings as well as in tramways and the interesting devolvement of some of the companies affected by the nationalisation of electricity undertakings is dealt with briefly in the following chapter.

Space precludes us from dealing in any but the most cursory manner with the history of any individual company – even the biggest of them all, Midland Red – but it is, perhaps, important to mention that even within the relatively small number of BET operators in the Midlands few had achieved their 1950 status without passing through a period of development considerably more complex than the outline of the group's origins that has been given here might suggest. The involvement of the pre-nationalisation railway companies is more relevant to the BTC group, possibly, but it would be misleading if it was left to be assumed that railway interests occurred only in those companies which became wholly-owned BTC subsidiaries. East Midland Motor Services, for example, had been owned jointly by the London Midland & Scottish and London & North Eastern Railways in 1929 but BET obtained a controlling 51% interest in 1930. The two railways had also acquired a 50% interest in Trent Motor Traction in 1929. Those railway interests survived until NBC was formed in 1969, passing successively into British Transport Commission and Transport Holding Company ownership before their ultimate acquisition, together with the BET elements in the respective companies, by the National Bus Co. Even the Birmingham & Midland Motor Omnibus Co, the ubiquitous Midland Red, was never, after 1930, purely a road transport undertaking within the BET group, affected only by the wishes of ordinary shareholders and the parent Company. In 1930 the London, Midland & Scottish Railway obtained a 30% share in Midland Red and the Great Western Railway a 20% share, those shares passing to the British Transport Commission in 1948 upon nationalisation of the railways. It was, indeed, the case that after the 1942 restructuring of the BET and Tilling Groups only a dozen or so of the more than 40 operating companies in the two groups had no railway company investment in their share capital.

Birmingham and Midland Motor Omnibus Co – Midland Red

Right:

It is difficult to avoid the use of superlatives in describing the operator known to generations not by its formal title, not by the name its vehicles carried for so long, but by the familiar, friendly, epithet 'Midland Red'. It operated on the grand scale, built whilst others merely bought, and led whilst others followed. Its activities are, fortunately, very thoroughly chronicled and its vehicles minutely catalogued, their enthusiastic followers recording everything the company might just have overlooked. There are, indeed, enough former Midland Red vehicles in preservation today to meet the operational needs of two or three small undertakings and more than, for example, Burton Corporation ever had available. Operating on that grand scale – the largest bus company in England – it was, perhaps, inevitable that very many vehicles would survive but that survival rate represents, too, the uniqueness of the company, the esteem in which it was held, and the admiration and affection commanded by its vehicles. Until it fell, eventually, inevitably, victim to the Daimler and the Leyland hordes the Midland Red had been a very special fleet indeed.

Possibly the last vehicle in the fleet still to carry the 'Midland Red' radiator badge, SOS FEDD No 2120 (EHA 252) was by April 1959 the oldest bus in passenger use. No 2120 had Brush 56-seat bodywork and was new in 1938. The photograph was taken on 7 September 1960, in Sutton Coldfield Garage shortly before setting off on the S60 Sutton Coldfield-Streetly-New Oscott-Sutton Coldfield circular service. *A. F. Porter*

Above:
Although taken in 1939, at Leicester, this vehicle, HA 9466 ('A' fleet No 1515 from 1944 onwards), a classic SOS CON built in 1934 with Brush 38-seat body, was to remain in service until 1956. In 1952 it was rebodied, the 'new' body coming from ON No 1633. *Midland Red*

Left:
Wartime vehicle shortages meant that even Midland Red received commercially produced buses. No 2440 (GHA 794) was one of nine Leyland Titan TD7s delivered in 1942 and one of three to carry Northern Counties 56-seat non-austerity bodywork. It was photographed in Wolverhampton in 1950 and was finally withdrawn in 1955. *Robert Mills*

Above:
Another small batch of vehicles diverted to Midland Red to meet operational vehicle shortages, six AEC Regents, had been intended for Coventry Corporaion. No 2444 (GHA 798) was one of that batch, all of which had Brush 59-seat bodies. It was photographed in High Bullen, Wednesbury, probably in the early 1950s, and, like 2440, was withdrawn in 1955. *Robert Mills*

Below:
Whilst beginning with the FEDD the modern double-deckers have each in their way characterised the company's fleet to some extent, the earlier REDD, introduced in 1932/3, was still in limited use until the early 1950s. No 1371 (HA 8016) stands at the Barley Mow, Solihull, on 8 May 1949, a few months before the date on which this book, strictly, opens. No 1371, built in 1932, had a 52-seat Eastern Counties body and was, in fact, withdrawn from service in 1950. *J. E. Cull*

Above:

It is arguable that the standard SOS front-entrance double-deck bus more than any other type characterised the Midland Red fleet. Certainly, in 1960, just before their withdrawal from public service early in 1961, the last few FEDDs in use – cossetted, on undemanding routes – were seen as that, the last survivors of a vanished era and one that they themselves had once so characterised. FEDD No 2254 (FHA 236), built in 1939 but with refurbished 56-seat Brush bodywork, turns into Pinfold Street, Katherine's Cross, Darlaston, on a local service on 12 September 1960.   *A. F. Porter*

Below:

A once familiar scene but even the garage is closed now, no longer needed by West Midlands PTE, to whom it passed, with routes and vehicles, in the 1973 absorption of Midland Red's West Midlands local services. The place is Sutton Coldfield and on the forecourt on 31 March 1961 are Midland Red Type S6 No 3058 (HHA 659), Type S12 No 3745 (NHA 745) and Type S13 (Mark II) No 3939 (OHA 939). No 3058 was built in 1947 and had a 40-seat body by Metro-Cammell, extended to 44-seats by Roe in 1953, No 3745 was built in 1950 and had a Brush 44-seat body, and 3939 was built in 1952 and had a Brush 44-seat dual-purpose body.   *A. F. Porter*

Above:

The deceptiveness of Midland Red's house style is fairly apparent in this photograph of two quite different types. No 3135 (JHA 36) was an AEC Regent – Midland Red Type AD2 – built in 1950 and 3494 (MHA 494) was Midland Red's own Type D5, built in 1949. Both had Brush 56-seat bodies, that on 3494 being 8ft wide. A casual glance might well have suggested that they were, in fact, identical. The photograph was taken at Dudley, in Fisher Street, on 9 May 1961. *A. F. Porter*

Left:

Company policy dictated that other chassis builders' products were acquired only when BMMO's own workshops could not satisfy demand. Wartime conditions had seen the arrival of AECs, Daimlers, Guys and Leylands but postwar conditions also necessitated the purchase of chassis from other builders. AEC Regents were placed in service in 1949 and 1950, Guy Arabs in 1949, and Leyland PD2/20s – Midland Red Type LD8 – in 1952 and 1953. Although a few vehicles passed into BMMO ownership with the acquisition of independent operators in the 1950s, it was to be another 10 years before the company again had to turn to outside manufacturers to meet its needs. The Leyland PD2/20s, or LD8s, all with Leyland 56-seat bodies, were themselves, however, subjected to Midland Red styling requirements and the 'Midland Red look' was adopted for some time in its production of PD2s for other operators. No 4023 (SHA 423) seen here in Warwick Road, Acocks Green, Birmingham, on 30 March 1962, was, like all but the first LD8, built in 1953. *A. F. Porter*

Right:

The underfloor-engine double-decker was almost unique to Midland Red amongst British chassis builders until very recently, although AEC produced an underfloor-engined Regent IV which never went into production. Two vehicles were built by BMMO, Nos 4943 and 4944, in 1961, with 78 and 65-seat integral bodies by the company, the much lower seating capacity of 4944 being caused by a second stairway and a rear exit, as well as front entrance. These features were later removed and the seating capacity increased in 4944 to 77. Although several features, including the integral construction, were shared with the company's successful D9, built from 1960 to 1966, following the introduction of the D9 prototype in 1958, no further D10s were built. No 4944 (1944 HA) was photographed at High Bullen, Wednesbury, on the Wednesbury to Stourbridge service on 8 June 1961, just a few weeks after entering service. *A. F. Porter*

Below:

Whilst production of the D9 as the company's standard double-decker was to continue until 1966, a new standard vehicle in the form of the Daimler Fleetline made its appearance in the fleet in 1963. The CRG6 – Midland Red Type DD11 – like its stablemates in the Birmingham City fleet was to change the image of the Midland Red double-decker for ever. The reign of the company's own postwar double-deckers had been relatively short, seen in retrospect, and it is curious to reflect that only two years separated the elimination from passenger service of the last of the SOS FEDDs and the arrival of the first Alexander-bodied Fleetlines. Alexander-bodied 77-seat 5274 (5274 HA), new in 1963, calls at Coventry Pool Meadow bus station in the mid-1960s. *A. A. Cooper/T. W. Moore collection*

Left:
1962 saw the introduction of the first Leyland Leopard PSU3/ 4Rs to the Midland Red fleet with 53-seat – or dual-purpose 48-seat – bodies by Willowbrook or Weymann. These were classified by the Company as type LS18 or LS18A, later to be known simply as S18 or S18A. They were the first of very many Leopards to enter the fleet, some of the subsequent vehicles doing so by the acquisition of independent concerns. No 5841 (JHA 841E) was a member of a small batch of Leopards designated LS20 and delivered in December 1966 with Willowbrook dual-purpose 49-seat bodywork. They were intended, when introduced, to be used on light stage-carriage work on week-days and on coach duties at weekends and for that reason were regarded as semi-coaches. No 5841 was photographed on express service in Pool Meadow bus station, Coventry, not long after entering service in March 1967. *T. W. Moore*

Left:
The production of the Company's own single-decker models continued well after the completion of the last D9 in 1966, the last of the S23s, No 5991, not being completed until 1970. An earlier BMMO design to be built in large numbers was the S17, a 36ft single-decker introduced in 1963 and in production until the end of 1966. No 5682 (CHA 682C) was a Plaxton-bodied 52-seat vehicle placed in service in autumn 1965. It was photographed in Allesley, Warwickshire, in May 1966.   *T. W. Moore*

Below:
No 4559 (559 AHA) was one of nine BMMO S14s built with 40-seat bodies for one-man operation in 1956/57; others followed in 1957-59 and a few earlier vehicles were similarly converted. Most of the class, however, retained 42 or 43 seats when converted to one-man operation. No 4559 was photographed in Market Drayton on 30 April 1960. The other bus is Butter's HVO 920, an AEC Regal with 35-seat Willowbrook acquired by the Child's Ercall operator from Holt's of Manchester in 1959. It had originally been in service with East Midland Motor Services.   *A. F. Porter*

Bottom:
BMMO D9 No 4853 (853 KHA), fifth of the production batch of integrally-constructed 72-seat vehicles, swings past the shell of Birmingham's Market Hall on 31 August 1961. No 4853 was built in 1960, two years after the introduction of the prototype D9, No 4773.   *A. F. Porter*

929
SHREWSBURY
VIA SHAWBURY
MIDLAND
559 AHA

MIDLAND
176 TO BIRMINGHAM
VIA SHELDON
First Class fare
Crawford's
CREAM CRACKERS
MIDLAND
853 KHA

East Midlands Motor Services

Above:
The last 20 years of its existence as a BET company saw East Midland with a rather mixed fleet, though one in which Weymann and Leyland- bodied Leyland vehicles, of various chassis types, predominated for several years. In the early 1960s the fleet had more PD2/1s than any other type and D70 (KRR 70) belonged to the largest batch, 25 all-Leyland vehicles with 53-seat lowbridge bodies built in 1949/50. It stood at the Dog & Duck, Old Clipstone, near Mansfield, on 31 August 1962. Driver Bilby and his conductor pose in summer uniforms.   *A. F. Porter*

Left:
A little more modern by a few years and fitted with the Midland Red-influenced grille, this Leyland PD2/21, D111 (UNN 111) in the East Midland fleet, built in 1956 and fitted with a 59-seat Weymann body, waits in the bus station, Derby, on 23 September 1962, to begin its run to Chesterfield, the Company's headquarters.   *A. F. Porter*

Above:

No D183 (GNN 183D) was an Albion-Leyland Lowlander with Metro-Cammell 70-seat bodywork built in 1966. In this Nottingham bus station scene D183 waits to leave for Chesterfield on the service operated jointly with Trent. It was photographed in June 1969.   *G. H. F. Atkins*

Below:

With the relaxation of restrictions on the sale of Bristol and Eastern Coach Works products the almost inevitable association of Bristol chassis and Eastern Coach Works body became a thing of the past. East Midland's No O528 (UNN 528G) represented a combination which would have been unthinkable a few years earlier; it was a Bristol LH6L with Willowbrook 45-seat bodywork, one of a batch of 10 built in 1969. It was photographed in Nottingham in June 1969, when new.   *G. H. F. Atkins*

City of Oxford Motor Services

Above:
By 1961 the oldest double-deckers in the Oxford fleet were a small batch of AEC Regent IIIs new in 1948/49 with Northern Coachbuilders' 53-seat lowbridge bodywork. Here L142 (NWL 716), a member of that batch, is manoeuvring, probably in the mid-1950s. Very few non-AEC types were bought before 1961, when five Dennis Lolines were placed in service. *Roy Marshall*

Below:
The last four AEC Renowns to be built received Northern Counties 65-seat bodies and were delivered to the City of Oxford undertaking in 1967, perpetuating the AEC preference but using Northern Counties bodywork for the first time. No 369 (FWL 369E) the second of the batch, was brand-new when photographed. *Roy Marshall*

Above:
Northern Counties bodywork was used, though not exclusively, when the company turned to Daimler and the Fleetline. In this view the first of a 1969 batch of CRG6LX dual-doorway 70-seat buses is seen in High Street in April 1971, still in pre-NBC livery. No 382 (MJO 382H) is followed by No 381 (KFC 381G), an earlier Northern Counties Fleetline still in its original livery.   *T. W. Moore*

Potteries Motor Traction

Below:
PMT displayed a penchant for variety and another for the economic rebodying of sound vehicles in its fleet. No 265 (DVT 904) (destined to become L 60 in 1953) was a Leyland TD4 new to the company in 1936, when it carried Brush 56-seat lowbridge bodywork. That body was still carried when this photograph was taken, in Newcastle-under-Lyme, probably around 1950. In 1951, however, 265 was provided with a sumptuous new 8ft wide Northern Counties 53-seat body, itself to pass in 1956 to Leyland OPD2/1 SN450 (NEH 450).   *Roy Marshall collection*

Above:
Variety in the PMT fleet was not achieved only by the purchase of independent operators' businesses. Many small batches of vehicles were placed in service by the company, and several individual vehicles too. C5623 (VEH 623) was a Beadle-Commer T48B integral with 41-seat bodywork, new in 1955, and was photographed at Newcastle garage on 5 October 1962.   *A. F. Porter*

Below:
Many of the stage carriage services in the Potteries remained for many years in the hands of independent licensed operators and some still elude PMT takeover. Other independent operators, however, lost their identities many years ago, some by direct acquisition by PMT (or under its earlier identity of Potteries Electric Traction) and some by sale to other independents. One major independent which grew remarkably by the acquisition process, acquiring 16 independents in the 15 years which passed between its formation in 1929 and its own eventual acquisition by PMT in 1944, was Associated Bus Companies Ltd of Hanley. In this scene at Burslem garage on 21 August 1960, a former ABC Guy Arab I, L226 (JEH 260), new to ABC in 1942 and rebodied by Northern Counties in 1954, shares the yard with another former independent vehicle, L284 (KEH 7), a Daimler CWA6 new to Brown's Motor Co (Tunstall) Ltd in 1946, acquired with that undertaking's assets in 1951 and, like L226, rebodied by Northern Counties in 1954. The other bus is H530 (REH 530), an AEC Regent III with Northern Counties 58-seat body new to Potteries in 1953.   *A. F. Porter*

Above:
Not easily distinguishable from L226 L223, like L226, was rebodied by Northern Counties in 1954. L223 (JEH 111) was a Guy Arab I new to PMT in 1942 and when this photograph was taken on 17 July 1962 at Longton bus station it was the oldest bus in the PMT fleet. The other vehicle in the picture, sharing the backs to the sun pose, is L340 (LEH 748), a Leyland PD2/1 new to PMT in 1948. It carried a 53-seat lowbridge body built by Northern Counties.   *A. F. Porter*

Below:
Also a rebody was L458 (NEH 458), one of 24 export-type Leyland OPD2/1s placed in service in 1950, unusually, with Weymann 35-seat single-deck bodies. All were rebodied between 1954 and 1956, 14 of them receiving double-deck bodies from other vehicles and the remainder, including L458, receiving new 1954 53-seat Northern Counties double-deck bodies. It was photographed in Tower Square, Tunstall, on 21 August 1960.   *A. F. Porter*

PARK DRIVE
HANLEY STOKE SIN
29 MAY BANK RILEY ARMS
CIRCULAR
L 510
WVT 330

LICHFIELD
26 STONE COLWICH
DULUX
PMT
842 KVT

Left:
Amongst the miscellany of vehicles acquired by PMT when it took over the operations of Baxter (Hanley) Ltd in 1958 was Leyland PD2/20 WVT 330. This vehicle was allocated fleet No L510 by PMT, somewhat out of sequence with the number series that were current in 1958 for new vehicles. L510, grille modelled on that of the Midland Red LD8, a customised PD2/20 (see page 48), had been built in 1955 and had a Willowbrook 55-seat body. It was photographed standing in Parliament Square, Hanley, on 6 April 1962.   *A. F. Porter*

Below left:
Although the presence of former independents' vehicles, was for many years a characteristic of the PMT fleet the company regularly purchased batches of new vehicles. Standardisation might not have been prominent, but neither was conservatism and the excessive caution which standardisation can occasionally represent. PMT was amongst the earlier purchasers of the Leyland Atlantean, buying 75 Weymann-bodied 73-seat vehicles in two batches in 1959 and 1960. A few of these were, indeed, to remain in service for more than 20 years. No 842 (842 KVT) of the 1960 batch waits to return to duty in a car park at Lichfield on 23 September 1962.   *A. F. Porter*

Above:
A new arrival in the PMT fleet when this photograph was taken, No C916 (916 UVT) was one of 15 Leyland Leopard PSU3/3Rs placed in service in 1962. Ten had Willowbrook 54-seat bus bodies and five, of which No C916 was one, had 48-seat coach bodies by Plaxton. It was seen on touring duty in a public car park in Lichfield on 9 June 1962.   *A. F. Porter*

Below:
PMT acquired a single Daimler Roadliner, No SN1000 (6000 EH), a Marshall-bodied version, in 1964. That vehicle, which had been exhibited at the Earl's Court Show that autumn, was the first Roadliner to enter an operator's fleet. Two years were to pass before PMT placed a production batch in service, beginning in December, 1966. These were bodied by Plaxton and, like SN1000, had 50-seat bodywork. A coach-bodied version followed with 49-seat Plaxton bodywork and, a few months later came more, this time with Duple bodywork. No C1101 (PVT 101F), one of the latter, is seen taking a break in Leicester in June 1968 en route to Great Yarmouth.   *G. H. F. Atkins*

FLOWERS BITTER
STRATFORD BLUE
ALVESTON
38
CUE 244

STRATFORD BLUE
JUSTINS AVENUE
For the best pale ale
Pick FLOWERS BREWMASTER
TNX 454

Stratford-upon-Avon Blue Motors

Above left:
Until its total absorption by Midland Red in 1971 Stratford Blue – as it declared itself to the world – had for some 36 years been a wholly-owned but operationally independent subsidiary of the Birmingham and Midland Motor Omnibus Co. That fact of ownership, an incident of company law, could readily pass un-noticed, so little did the offspring turn to its monolithic parent for guidance or advice – or, for that matter, advantage. As an independently-operated subsidiary it had the appearance of a BET operator no more closely associated with Midland Red than was Potteries Motor Traction, say, or City of Oxford Motor Services, whose vehicles rolled into Stratford on a stage carriage service, via Chipping Norton and Shipston-on-Stour, of the two companies' joint operation. During its many years of seeming independence only three BMMO vehicles were acquired, Stratford Blue being free to pursue its own preferences, largely standardising on Tilling-Stevens products until after the war, when it switched its allegiance to Leyland. Here No 38 (GUE 244), a Leyland PD2/1 built in 1948 and fitted with a 56-seat Leyland body, pauses in Bridge Street, Stratford, on 15 April 1961.   *A. F. Porter*

Left:
A few minutes after No 38 was photographed in Bridge Street, the bus station provided a pair of later PD2/12s. No 20 (TNX 454) was built in 1956 and had Willowbrook 63-seat bodywork and No 24 (MAC 571), largely obscured by its handsome stable-mate, was built four years earlier and carried a 58-seat Leyland body.   *A. F. Porter*

Above:
In another Stratford bus station scene on 15 April 1961, the last of Stratford Blue's all-Leyland PD2/1s, No 31 (JUE 359), built in 1950, shares standage with 46 (3946 UE), a Park Royal 45-seat-bodied Leyland Tiger Cub PSUC1/1 built in 1960.   *A. F. Porter*

Trent Motor Traction

Below:
Like Potteries Motor Traction – and, indeed, Northern General Transport, Sunderland District, and one or two other group members in north-east England – Trent was for a time in the 1920s and 1930s supplied with vehicles largely by BMMO whose Carlyle Works SOS types were as familiar outside Midland Red territory in parts of the Midlands and the North East as they were in Smethwick. No 1010 (RC 3332) was one of the 100 FEDDs built in 1935, 15 of them going to Trent. It had Metro-Cammell 56-seat bodywork and was withdrawn with the rest of the batch (No 1002 having burnt out in 1948) in 1949. The photograph was probably taken in Derby shortly before the vehicle was withdrawn.   *R. F. Mack*

Above:
Before 1963, apart from the remaining SOS types, the Trent fleet had for some years been limited to Leyland and AEC products. Photographed on one of the Manchester express services, probably in the early 1950s but at an unknown location, is AEC Regal 706 (RC 4607), new in 1937. It has a Willowbrook 1950 35-seat body.   *R. H. G. Simpson*

Below:
Whilst the preference for Leyland and AEC types was still evident in the Trent fleet there was also a noticeable preference for the bodywork of a few manufacturers, Willowbrook being well to the fore amongst those so favoured. In this AEC/Willowbrook combination two dual-purpose vehicles, Nos 103 and 105 (BRC 303/5) wait in Derby for their private hire passengers on 31 July 1960. Both were Regal IIIs and had 33-seat bodies.   *A. F. Porter*

Above:
Two more types sharing the company-favoured Willowbrook bodywork are seen in this quiet spot in Derby bus station on 8 October 1962. They are AEC Regent II No 1142 (ACH 632), one of a batch of 43 56-seat vehicles built from 1946 to 1948, and Leyland Tiger Cub PSUC1/2T 148 (HRC 148), a 1956 vehicle with 41-seat dual-purpose bodywork.   *A. F. Porter*

Below:
Another of the same batch as 1142, No 1135 (RC 9651) shares a platform at Derby bus station on 31 July 1960, with 1947-built Regal II No 759 (RC 9686), another Willowbrook-bodied vehicle, seating 35.   *A. F. Porter*

Above:
This Leyland Tiger Cub PSUC1/1T, No 819, later 369 (FCH 19), was unusual in the Trent fleet in carrying Saunders-Roe bodywork, built in 1954 and seating 44. It was photographed in Wetmore Road bus station in Burton-on-Trent on 11 September 1961.   *A. F. Porter*

Above right:
Like its near neighbour, Potteries Motor Traction, Trent was relatively quick to put the Leyland Atlantean into service, with a Weymann-bodied 73-seat batch of 20 entering service in 1959 and 1960. The first of these was No 1358 (ORC 758), renumbered 600 in 1962. This vehicle, then recently renumbered 600, is seen here in Wetmore Road bus station, Burton-on-Trent, on 8 October 1962, sharing the tarmac with Stevenson's No 9 (HTF 822), an ex-Accrington Corporation all-Leyland PD2/1.   *A. F. Porter*

North Western Road Car Company

Right:
Unlike the other BET companies represented in this section, the North Western Road Car Co was based outside the 'Midlands'. It was, nevertheless, though organised from Stockport, an operator of some significance in North Derbyshire and had stage carriage routes that penetrated further south as well as into Lancashire and Yorkshire. Some long distance services were shared with Trent and with other operators from outside the Midlands. This Atkinson, No 504 (FDB 504), was on the joint service to Manchester when photographed in Derby bus station on 23 September 1962. The Atkinson chassis, so well-known in freight haulage, was not often bought by public service vehicle operators and in the 13 years of construction fewer than 120 chassis were bought by British operators. North Western had a total of 16 Atkinsons, including the first two to be built, and would have liked to have seen this rugged and economical type become a BET standard, but it was not to be. No 504 was a PM746H and had Weymann 42-seat rear-entrance bodywork. It was new in 1952.   *A. F. Porter*

HATTON 1b

TARANTELLA

600

ORC 758

STEVENSONS

MTF 822

T.V. TIME FOR SWEETS JOHN HORN'S OF COURSE

NORTH WESTERN

504

FDB 504

X1

The British Transport Commission Group of Companies

Unlike British Electric Traction, which has had a corporate existence from 1895, the British Transport Commission was a creature of statute that lasted only from 1948 to 1962 as a corporate entity. Its transport interests were manifold and even in the sphere of road passenger transport its roles were varied; most of the operating bus companies in which the Transport Commission held an interest, either on its formation in 1948 – all the Tilling Group's bus companies were acquired in September 1948, nine months after the Commission's creation – or subsequently, were wholly-owned but it also had shares inherited from the pre- nationalisation railway companies in some bus companies that were to remain in BET control until the formation of the National Bus Co in 1969.

The British Transport Commission was created under the provisions of the Transport Act, 1947, and the ownership of the bus companies which were acquired in 1948, and subsequently, was vested in it. Rationalisation of this somewhat cumbersome form of ownership and control came in 1962 when, upon the dissolution of the Transport Commission under the provisions of the 1962 Transport Act, ownership and control of the nationalised bus companies was vested in the Transport Holding Company. The THC functioned in the public sector much as BET functioned in the private. Day-to-day operational control remained with the operating companies themselves and to the ordinary travelling public there was no sign whatever that any fundamental change in the organisation of the nationalised element of the industry had taken place.

The bulk of the British Transport Commission holdings were acquired with the purchase of the Tilling group companies in 1948, some 21 undertakings being included in the acquisition. With these went Eastern Coach Works, the wholly-owned coachbuilding subsidiary of Eastern Counties Omnibus Co, and the chassis-manufacturing element of the Bristol Tramways and Carriage Co. The products of both concerns had long been favoured by the Tilling group but they had also manufactured for the general, non-Tilling, market. A prohibition on the manufacture of equipment for anything other than its own operations – a provision of the Transport Act, 1947 – precluded the newly-nationalised transport undertakings and their manufacturing constituents from further commercial construction for several years and during this period, which ended in 1965 with the acquisition by British Leyland of a 25% holding in Bristol Commercial Vehicles – the manufacturing subsidiary established in 1955 – many of the BTC/THC companies completely standardised their fleets on Bristol chassis and Eastern Coach Works bodies. The 'Bristol-look', so different from the visual characteristics of the municipalities, the BET Group companies and the independents, made the BTC/THC companies instantly recognisable, whatever livery they carried. The Midlands had, in fact, only Cheltenham District Traction – a Bristol Omnibus Co subsidiary – Mansfield District Traction, Midland General, Nottinghamshire & Derbyshire Traction, and the United Counties Omnibus Co based within its perimeters – though other BTC companies had services to the Midlands or within those perimeters. Curiously, of those Midlands-based companies only United Counties had been a Tilling group operator; the others came into BTC possession by much more circuitous routes.

Cheltenham District was acquired by the Transport Commission with the operations of the Red & White group in 1950, passing to the Bristol organisation as an operational convenience. South Midland Motor Services of Oxford was included in the same acquisition and was transferred to Thames Valley as that BTC company's coaching service, retaining the Oxford base. Mansfield District, Midland General and Nottinghamshire & Derbyshire Traction were owned by the Midland Counties Electric Supply Co, a Balfour Beatty group subsidiary, and passed into the ownership of the British Electricity Authority on the nationalisation of electricity undertakings in 1948. A more detailed account of these companies and their relationships is given in the appropriate captions.

All THC operators in existence at the time became constituent companies of the new parent NBC on its creation on 1 January 1969, joining the newly-acquired BET group of companies in the much enlarged and now very familiar nationalised sector of the industry. The West Riding Automobile Co was the last of the major independents to join the THC fold before the creation of the NBC. It did so in 1967.

Cheltenham District Traction Company

Above:
Whilst being a wholly-owned subsidiary of the Bristol Omnibus Co, Cheltenham District kept its independent image for several years after the 1950/51 rationalisation of BTC companies under which, as a member of the Red & White group, it had passed into Bristol control. The Bristol Company's structure had always been complex, and its relationship with local authorities a little unusual, but wherever it operated, apart from Cheltenham, its vehicles, even when carrying the 'Bath Services' legend, were quite unmistakably part of the Bristol Omnibus stable. It was not so, however, with the Cheltenham subsidiary; that was, even with the Bristol/ECW vehicles in the fleet, no more

obviously a Bristol Omnibus operation than was the wholly separate Red & White itself. Red & White sold all its group undertakings – including 10 separate operating companies, Red & White, Cheltenham District and South Midland amongst them – to the state in 1950. Rationalisation was immediately necessary and the Cheltenham District subsidiary, which Red & White had itself acquired from the Balfour Beatty group only in 1939, passed into Bristol Omnibus Company control, remaining in separate management, and with its own distinctive livery, for several years. From its years as a Red & White subsidiary Cheltenham District Traction took several distinctly non-Bristol vehicles into the Bristol group, including AECs, Guys, and Albions. In this picture Albion CX19 No 73 (FCY 763), with a Metro-Cammell 56-seat body, stands in the town centre at Cheltenham on 30 August 1960. No 73 was placed in service in 1949. *A. F. Porter*

WHITE
WHITES
NHY
938
HESTER'S WAY
5
Chelt

THE
GLOBE
INN
THE GLOB
J.G.SHENTON LTD for The Latest in MEN'S WEAR
HIGH STREET (Opposite Fleece Hotel)
RESTBURY
CENTRE
OAKLANDS
WAR MEMORIAL
CHELTENHAM DISTRICT
94
WHY
945

Below left:
The arrival of the Bristol Lodekka in the Cheltenham fleet in
1956 signalled, perhaps more than anything, the parent
Bristol Omnibus Co's influence in the affairs of the subsidiary
and the beginning of the end of Cheltenham's seemingly
separate existence. No 94 (WHY 945) was the first of the
Lodekkas to join the Cheltenham fleet and here stands
driverless in North Street, Cheltenham, on the day in August
1960 that Nos 73 and 80 were photographed.

Nos 80 and 94 were with the rest of the District fleet,
renumbered into the main Bristol Omnibus Co's fleet in 1966,
becoming L8551 and L8565 respectively. New vehicles for
the Cheltenham fleet had already for some time been placed
in service with numbers in the parent company's fleet,
although the subsidiary's maroon livery persisted. A
reversion to an earlier kind of autonomy, though within NBC
structures, was to come about 17 years later when, in 1983,
the Cheltenham and Gloucester Omnibus Co Ltd was
formed, taking 160 vehicles from the Bristol fleet.
Cheltenham District Traction's modest 30-odd vehicles of
the early 1960s had been, perhaps if only in a presumptive
sense, the embryo of that much-expanded undertaking.
Whilst Birmingham, West Bromwich, Walsall,
Wolverhampton and Coventry all fell tiny well-held
Cheltenham lives on.   A. F. Porter

Mansfield District Traction Company

Below:
It is not intended that this album should be seen as an
historical account of the transport undertakings which it
illustrates, or of their fleets. It would be impossible, however,
to give a reasonably balanced impression of those
undertakings without the occasional mention of significant
background facts, and it seems appropriate here to refer to
the close relationship that once existed between Mansfield
District Traction, the Midland General Omnibus Co, and the
Nottinghamshire & Derbyshire Traction Co. With quite
separate origins rooted in the tramway operations of,
respectively, the Mansfield & District Light Railway Co and
the Nottinghamshire & Derbyshire Tramways Co the three
bus companies were eventually acquired by the Midland
Counties Electric Supply Co, Midland General having been
incorporated in 1920 as a subsidiary of what was by then the
Nottinghamshire & Derbyshire Traction Co. With the
nationalisation of electricity undertakings in 1948 the three
bus companies passed briefly into the ownership of the
British Electricity Authority as part of Midland Counties
Electricity's assets, but on 1 April 1948 they passed into
British Transport Commission ownership, having been
assets not wholly compatible with the Electricity Authority's
primary responsibility. There they remained, closely
associated, with Midland General growing and Notts &
Derby declining in importance until it was the subordinate of
the two, and with the occasional transfer of vehicles taking
place between Mansfield District, Midland General, and
Notts & Derby, until their absorption into the National Bus
Company organisation in 1968. Now, of course, all has
changed. Notts & Derby was lost in the Midland General
operation and Midland General itself fell under Trent Motor
Traction control in 1972. Mansfield District was absorbed
into the East Midland Motor Services operation at the same
time.

In this illustration, probably taken in the mid-1960s, Bristol
MW6G No 290 (373RNN), new in 1963 and with ECW 39-seat
coachwork, stands discreet. It could be at a Spa, or
Blackpool.   *Roy Marshall*

Above:

The closeness of the operating companies became more apparent in 1966 when certain vehicles in the Midland General and Mansfield District fleets began to carry both fleet titles. In this picture Mansfield District No 217 (KNN 611E), clearly on private hire duty, though at an unknown location, shows them both. No 217 was a Bedford VAM new in 1967 and carried Duple Viceroy 41-seat coachwork.   *Robert Mack collection*

Below:

Amongst the first vehicles introduced by the company after its becoming a NBC subsidiary were nine Bristol RELL6HLXs with ECW 44-seat bodywork. No A140 (DRA 351G) was new in 1969 and was photographed some years later in NBC livery.   *Robert Mack*

Midland General Omnibus Company

Above:

Whilst in BTC ownership, then as subsidiaries of the THC until the formation of the NBC, Mansfield District and the two Midland General companies came, as might be expected, very much to resemble the BTC undertakings in other parts of the country, wholly dominated by Bristol chassis types and Eastern Coach Works bodies. Pre-standardisation vehicles, however, survived for many years after the old Midland Counties Electricity trio of bus companies was nationalised. Leyland TS8 No 153 (FRB 717), standing in Nottingham in September 1955, had been new in 1939 and carried Weymann dual-purpose 35-seat bodywork. It was withdrawn from service in 1958. *G. H. F. Atkins*

Below:

Built a decade after TS8 No 153 and following nationalisation, AEC Regal III No 182 (KRR 271), transferred in 1958 from the Mansfield District fleet where it had entered service as that company's No 25, looks with its Weymann 35-seat bodywork anything but a member of the Bristol-dominated BTC group of operators' fleets. The photograph was taken near the entrance to the Crich Tramway Museum – now the National Tramway Museum – on 12 June 1962, some nine years after the first Bristol chassis bus was placed in service by this small group of closely associated BTC companies. *A. F. Porter*

Left:

Like most of the BTC companies the familiar combination of Bristol chassis and ECW bodywork gave the Mansfield, Midland General and Notts & Derby group an appearance that, despite the survival of many non-Bristol vehicles, very quickly came to resemble – livery apart, perhaps – any BTC company from United Automobile Services in the north-east to Southern and Western National in the south-west. The introduction of the Lodekka FSF6G with 60-seat forward-entrance ECW bodywork in 1961 kept up the pace of assimilation of the parent group's policy and image. Brand-new FSF6G No 506 (446 SNU) stands, somewhat shamed by its surroundings, in Mount Street bus station, Nottingham, on 31 March 1962.   *A. F. Porter*

Nottinghamshire & Derbyshire Traction Company

Below:

The composite image of the Mansfield, Midland General and Notts & Derby group might well be conveyed by the photograph of Notts & Derby No 309 (SRB 537), one of the 1953 batch of KSW6Gs with 60-seat bodies that introduced the Bristol chassis to the fleet, and Midland General No 34 (JNU 374), a 1945 Guy Arab with much-improved Northern Counties 56-seat utility bodywork. Nos 309 and 34 were photographed in a quiet corner of Mount Street bus station, Nottingham, on 2 April 1961.   *A. F. Porter*

Above right:

Platform 4 of Mount Street bus station in Nottingham was as run-down as any other part of the precinct when this picture was taken but had at least this sylvan corner to set off the familiar lines of what was to be, by 1965, the almost exclusively Bristol fleet of the Notts & Derby subsidiary. When this picture was taken on 31 July 1960, however, it still had a dozen Regent IIIs, one of them a former Mansfield District vehicle. No 471 (20 DRB), one of a batch of 10 built in 1957-58, was a 58-seat rear-entrance Bristol LD6G. Midland General had 45 and Mansfield District 25 58-seat LD6Gs built between 1954 and 1959, similar to 471.   *A. F. Porter*

United Counties Omnibus Company

Below:
United Counties had its origins in an extremely 'independent' operation but became part of the Tilling group in 1931 and, of course, a BTC company in 1948. United Counties, like its predecessors, has always been based in Northamptonshire but as its operations expanded services reached the surrounding counties of Huntingdonshire, Cambridgeshire, Bedfordshire, Hertfordshire, Buckinghamshire, Oxfordshire, Leicestershire and Rutland. Unlike the adventures of companies in the Red & White group or the Midland General group, once Tilling control was established United Counties experienced nothing more traumatic than the absorption in 1952 of Eastern National's Midland Area operation and the acquisition of 239 Eastern National buses. At the same time United Counties lost the Oxford-London service to South Midland Motor Services and in 1962 transferred its own excursions and tours licences to Wallace Arnold. United Counties took over the Bedfordshire and Northamptonshire services of Birch Brothers, the London independent, in 1969 and in 1970 acquired the entire Luton Corporation undertaking.

By 1960 United Counties was wholly standardised on Bristol chassis and Eastern Coach Works bodies. Illustrating the UCOC operation of that period is, largely, illustrating a very typical BTC company. Some slight variation on that very basic theme is therefore offered in this photograph of No 817 (ONO 77), a 1950-built Bristol K5G with 55-seat ECW body, of which there were many in the UCOC fleet. It was, however, one of the former Eastern National vehicles acquired with that company's Midland Area operation in 1952. It was photographed in Northampton on 20 July 1962.   *A. F. Porter*

Bristol Omnibus Company

To include Bristol in a book devoted to the buses of the Midlands may seem to be stretching things to the limit, but it must be remembered that Bristol had stage-carriage services that reached as far north as Malvern Link in Worcestershire, as Evesham, jointly with Stratford Blue, and Oxford, jointly with City of Oxford.

The Bristol conglomerate of the 1950s and 1960s – and there is, perhaps, hardly a more appropriate epithet to describe the complex pattern of related company structures and working arrangements than 'conglomerate' – was exceedingly complex. Like many undertakings that were eventually to become bus companies Bristol Omnibus Co had its origins in street tramways. The Bristol Tramways Co opened its operations in 1875 with horse-drawn trams using street tracks leased from Bristol Corporation and, incidentally, thereby creating a relationship between the city and the company which persists to the present time; Bristol Corporation has, since 1875, depended entirely on a series of agreements with the company for the provision of transport services and has never itself provided them. Electric traction had completely replaced the horsetrams by 1900 and motorbus services began in 1906, progressively replacing horsebuses which had been introduced as feeders to the tramway system in 1877. The company, as the Bristol Tramways & Carriage Co Ltd – a name to be retained, indeed, until 1957 – was unusually enterprising and as well as establishing operating branches in Bath, Cheltenham, Gloucester, Wells, Weston-super-Mare, and Swindon by 1922 had already by 1909, commenced the building of both chassis and bus bodies. In 1929 control of the Bristol Tramways Co was acquired by the Great Western Railway but was transferred two years later to the Western National Omnibus Co, in which the Great Western Railway itself held a 50% interest (the other 50% being acquired by the Tilling group in the same year as part of its wider acquisition of the National Omnibus and Transport Co). With the nationalisation of the railway and Tilling group interests in 1948 the Bristol Tramways Co disposed of its remaining private holdings to the BTC, thus establishing the undertaking as a wholly-owned BTC company. The construction of vehicles continued but their sale was limited by the provisions of the Transport Act 1947 to companies in British Transport Commission ownership and in 1955 was separated from the operational activities of the Bristol Tramways Co.

Some rationalisation of services followed nationalisation, involving the acquisition of Cheltenham District, as already mentioned, and the rearrangement and transfer of some Gloucestershire services between Bristol, Western National and the reconstructed Red & White Motor Services.

This picture illustrates neatly the complexity of Bristol. Completely isolated from the main area of Bristol operations, though of course with connections to them, Bristol K No 3726 (LAE 303) waits to leave Cheltenham for Gloucester on service 49. This service, provided by the parent company, linked the separate operating territories of the autonomous Cheltenham District Traction Co and the special Gloucester City services operated by the parent company as a non-autonomous undertaking whose vehicles carried the Gloucester City crest. No 3726 was one of a batch placed in service between 1948 and 1950, and the photograph was taken at Cheltenham bus station on 10 August 1960.   *A. F. Porter*

Above:

In another service operating from Cheltenham 58-seat Lodekka L8278 (UHY 407), a 1955 vehicle, waits at Cirencester on 30 August 1960 en route to Swindon. *A. F. Porter*

Below:

Well inside Midland Red territory, on the service from Cheltenham operated jointly with Stratford Blue, L8464 (YHT 960), a 58-seat Lodekka from a 1957-59 batch, waits in High Street, Evesham, before returning to Cheltenham. The photograph was taken on 10 August 1960. *A. F. Porter*

Lincolnshire Road Car Company

Above:
The genealogy of transport undertakings is often as curiously complex as that of any individual. The Lincolnshire Road Car Co, included here by virtue of its services into Leicestershire and Nottinghamshire and a garage at Newark, had a Lincoln headquarters and services primarily confined to the county. Its origins, however, like those of United Automobile Services, lay in East Anglia. The Lincoln branch of the small Clacton & District concern was opened in 1922 but in 1928 passed into Tilling & British Automobile Traction ownership as the Lincolnshire Road Car Co. Lincolnshire remained within the Tilling Group until its nationalisation 20 years later and that period saw the Road Car Co undergo considerable expansion, beginning with the acquisition of the whole of United Automobile Services' operations in the county in 1931. The acquisition of very many independent operators before nationalisation, and several following it, meant that the Lincolnshire fleet has at times been far removed from the typical standardised Tilling and BTC company fleet and the almost total standardisation on Bristol/ECW products which Lincolnshire itself achieved by the early 1960s. Until 1939 the company preferred its new purchases to be Leyland – three TD1s new on the formal establishment of Lincolnshire in 1931 lasted until 1954 – but, after acquiring its first Bristols in 1944, standardised on that make from 1953 onwards.

In this scene on the Great North Road in Newark a Bristol L6B with 35-seat ECW body is just caught between moving vehicles on 31 August 1962. No 2018 (FFW 828) was new in 1949. *A. F. Porter*

Above right:
This view of Bristol SC4LK No 2457 (PFW 939), a 1958 vehicle with 35-seat ECW bodywork, was taken in Grantham on 26 June 1962, and is justified for inclusion here on the grounds that vehicles of two bona fide Midlands operators, Trent and Midland Red, have background roles. *A. F. Porter*

Right:
The reverse side of the coin is seen here in the form of Lincolnshire Lodekka LD6G No 2372 (NFE 935), a 60-seat vehicle and the last of the model to be built for the company, in 1959. It was photographed on 31 July 1960 in Huntingdon Street bus station, Nottingham, on the service to Grantham operated jointly with Trent. The Trent bus alongside is Leyland PD2/12 No 1247 (DRC 947), subsequently renumbered 737, one of an all-Leyland 58-seat batch built from 1953 to 1955.

DULUX
TRENT
31 DUPLICATE
DRINK BARNSLEY BREWERY'S BRIGHT ALES
LINCOLNSHIRE
PFE 939

Goodwins
Flour
65 P
CLIFTON
Goodwins
Flour
Make
Good Friends
with
MANSFIELD A
GRANTHAM
33
PLATFORM 7
GRANTHAM
TRENT & LINCS
BOTTESFORD
BARROWBY
BINGHAM
TRENT
RADCLIFFE
SAXONDALE HOSPITAL
CHESTERFIELD
TRENT & EAST
MIDLAND
EAST KIRKBY
MANSFIELD
PLEASLEY
GLAPWELL
SUTTON-IN-
ASHFIELD
TRENT
HUCKNALL
ANNESLEY
EAST KIRKBY
KIRKBY-in-ASHFIELD
DRC 947
FE
35

Red & White Motor Services

Red & White was based primarily in Monmouthshire and South Wales. But for its services in the Forest of Dean and to Gloucester – and, more remotely, its pre-BTC parentage of Cheltenham District Traction and South Midland Motor Services of Oxford – it could not properly find a place amongst Midlands operators. That series of historical accidents, if that is what they were, merits inclusion of a short mention of the company and one or two illustrations of its vehicles. The Red & White Group was, until the sale of its assets to the British Transport Commission in 1950, a major independent collection of transport companies which included Red & White Motor Services, United Welsh, Newbury & District, Venture, and several others as well as Cheltenham District and South Midland. Post-nationalisation rationalisation brought a change in the operating areas previously within the preserves of Red & White, Bristol, and Western National, under which Red & White and Western National both lost their Stroud garage and operations to Bristol and Bristol transferred its Coleford garage and Forest of Dean services to Red & White.

Some 10 years later Red & White Albion Valkyrie CX13 S5.48 (GWO 866) stands in Coleford railway station yard, in former Bristol Omnibus Company – more strictly, Bristol Tramways Company – shared territory. S5.48 had Lydney bodywork, was new in 1948, and was photographed on 13 May 1961.   *A. F. Porter*

South Midland Motor Services

South Midland had been an Oxford-based member of the Red & White Group, notable for its Oxford to London express coach services. Following nationalisation the British Transport Commission placed the South Midland operation (together with Newbury & District) into the hands of Thames Valley Traction, and it became the Thames Valley coaching operation, though still based in Oxford. South Midland vehicles were numbered in the Thames Valley fleet although they carried South Midland fleet names. Three years after the formation of the National Bus Co in 1968 South Midland joined City of Oxford Motor Services.

In this Victoria Coach Station park scene on 21 June 1962, No 94 (TWL 59) – a 1954 Bristol LS6B with 37-seat ECW body – has arrived in London from Oxford. Southdown No 1744 (8744 CD), standing alongside, was a brand-new Leyland Leopard L2, the last of a 1961/62 batch with Harrington 28-seat bodies.   *A. F. Porter*

Black & White Motorways

Below:
This coaching operator, a major contributor to the Associated Motorways network of services, began its operations from Cheltenham in 1926 as an independent concern but came, in 1930, into the joint ownership of Midland Red, City of Oxford Motor Services and Bristol. Of these owners Midland Red and Bristol (Greyhound) themselves became participants in the Associated Motorways operations with Black & White and with Eastern Counties, Lincolnshire, Red & White, Royal Blue and United Counties. The peculiar hybridity of Black & White Motorways, with its ownership drawn from both BET and BTC group companies, did not impede its operational efficiency or its position at the centre of the Associated Motorways network.

This photograph perhaps typifies both the Black & White operation and the wider Associated Motorways activity. In this picture, taken in a public car park in Paignton, Devon, on 27 May 1961, Black & White No 141 (KDF 992), a Leyland Royal Tiger PSU1/11 with Willowbrook coachwork, one of a batch of 31 built from 1951 to 1953, has arrived from Cheltenham to join Red & White's Bristol MW6G UC5.59 (UWO 705), new in 1959 and also on Associated Motorways duty for its owners.   *A. F. Porter*

Long Distance Coach Services

Most of the Midlands-based operators, other than the local authorities, have operated long distance coach services; indeed even amongst the municipal operators coaching services are not absolutely unknown. In addition to the outward-bound coach services of the Midlands operators, often operated jointly with other companies along the route, many services operated by companies based in other parts of the country, including Scotland, came in to Midlands destinations. Long distance tours from the south to northern and Scottish destinations, and from Scotland and the north to southern destinations, were hardly likely to reach those destinations without running up a considerable mileage on Midlands roads. Each of these, the scheduled services and the tours, brought a glimpse of the exotic. Southdown green, a most Regal Blue, West Yorkshire's Tilling red, East Yorkshire's pale blue, and a host of creams relieved by the most judicious touch of the operator's prime colour. Private hire – the one-off run – brought strange and startling sights occasionally, as it still does. Together, however, these coaching activities were an entertaining intrusion into the ordinarily observed highways of the Midlands and the familiar vehicles and liveries of the home-base operators. Something of their character comes across in the pictures chosen to represent them.

East Yorkshire Motor Services

Below left:

The long distance coach services into Birmingham brought many elegant, or spectacularly ornate, vehicles on to Midlands roads for very many years, although the quieter tastes of the 1950s and 1960s supplanted the baroque tendencies of earlier times. One of the more noticeable features of these coaching services was the procession of vehicles coming southwards from the East and West Ridings of Yorkshire as the collective 'Yorkshire Services'. Yorkshire Services was an association of East Midland, East Yorkshire, West Yorkshire, Yorkshire Traction and Yorkshire Woollen District, co-operating across BET and BTC group lines in the long-haul business, operating services to London and to the East and West Midlands that were separate from their individual company long-distance services.

East Yorkshire 733 (9733 AT), a 1962 Leyland Leopard PSU3/1R with Willowbrook dual-purpose 47-seat body is caught arriving in Sutton Coldfield on 30 June 1962, a mere six miles or so to go.   *A. F. Porter*

West Yorkshire Road Car Company

Above:

The West Yorkshire contribution to the Yorkshire Services operation was, as a BTC subsidiary, invariably a Bristol vehicle. Here dual-purpose LS5G No SUG43 (OWX 155), one of a large batch of mostly 41-seaters built between 1953 and 1958, comes into Sutton Coldfield on 15 August 1961.   *A. F. Porter*

Yorkshire Traction Company

Below:

Yorkshire Traction's contribution to the pool on 9 June 1962 was Leyland Tiger Cub PSUC1/2 No 1029 (HHE 180). No 1029 was one of 11 such vehicles built in 1954/55 and had Willowbrook 39-seat bodywork. It was photographed arriving at the Parade, Sutton Coldfield.   *A. F. Porter*

Yorkshire Woollen District Transport Company

Above:
Hardly inviting praise for the sensitivity of its lines or for the thoughtfulness of committing so old a vehicle to the arduous run to Birmingham, Yorkshire Woollen No 740 (HD 9148) was, nevertheless, only 11 years old when this photograph was taken on 16 June 1962. No 740 was a Leyland Royal Tiger PSU1/15, one of a batch of six built in 1951 with Windover 39-seat coachwork. It was photographed approaching Sutton Coldfield from Lichfield. *A. F. Porter*

Northern General Transport Company

Below:
Not on a mystery tour in County Durham but, in fact, on a scheduled long-distance service nearing its end, Northern General AEC Reliance 1720 (FCN 720) with Willowbrook dual-purpose bodywork enters Sutton Coldfield at a modest speed on 12 August 1961. It had left Newcastle upon Tyne at 8.30am on the Yorkshire Services 'Ten Cities Express' and was due at Pool Meadow, Coventry, at 7.13pm. *A. F. Porter*

Ribble Motor Services

Above:

Glasgow to Coventry before the motorways arrived was a demanding route requiring stamina on everyone's part. The best that could be expected was a journey time of a little under 15 hours and more than adequate, nowadays, for a flight from Heathrow to Delhi via the scenic all-stops Gulf States route. Showing nothing of the rigours of such a journey Leyland Royal Tiger PSU1/15 No 821 (DRN 743) stands quietly in Pool Meadow, Coventry, on 13 August 1962 alongside Red & White Motor Services UC1.62 (101 CWO). No 821 was, like Yorkshire Woollen District's 740, a 1951 Leyland Royal Tiger PSU1/15 but carried a Leyland 41-seat body. Red & White's UC1.62, in from Cardiff, was the first of that company's new-style Bristol MW6Gs with 39-seat ECW bodywork and had been placed in service earlier in the **year.**   *A. F. Porter*

Scout Motor Services

Below:

Ribble acquired the Scout concern in 1962 and immediately began the process of repainting the fleet in its own livery. Caught at Pool Meadow, Coventry, before losing its Scout livery, however, was Ribble S58 (PRN 146), a Leyland Leopard L2 built in 1961 and carrying a Duple Donnington 38-seat – and toilet – body. The photograph, taken on 25 June 1962 with S58 preparing to return to its Preston Base, also includes Ribble's Blackpool coaching subsidiary, Standerwick's No 8 (NFR 956), a 1958 Leyland Tiger Cub PSUC1/2 with Burlingham Seagull 41-seat coachwork, loading for Blackpool, and Midland Red's D5B No 3782 (NHA 782), built in 1950 and carrying Brush 56-seat bodywork, but engaged in much less portentous duties.   *A. F. Porter*

W. C. Standerwick

Left:
Ribble's own long distance coaching services did not prevent it perpetuating the apparently separate, though wholly-owned, coaching services of W. C. Standerwick Ltd of Blackpool. The relationship with Scout Motor Services, too, was close and, until the acquisition of Scout by Ribble in 1962, Standerwick's services were advertised as 'Standerwick-Scout (in association with Ribble)'. Whilst covering much of the main trunk routes in common with Ribble, Standerwick operated essentially from Fleetwood, Blackpool and Keswick to Birmingham, Oxford and London. The opening of the first section of the M1 coincided approximately with the introduction of the Leyland Atlantean and Ribble obtained special motorway coach versions with additional facilities for its own operations and those of Standerwick. These became popularly known as 'Gay Hostesses'; they carried hostesses too, though the whole concept was subsequently abandoned with the introduction of motorway services. Wholly new in concept, of course, it has recently been revived! In this picture, Standerwick 29 (VFR 371), a 1961 'Gay Hostess' Leyland Atlantean PDR1/1 with Weymann 50-seat body, pulls into Digbeth bus station, Birmingham, en route from London to Keswick, via what relatively little of the motorway there then was. The photograph was taken on 14 February 1962.   *A. F. Porter*

Crosville Motor Services

Below:
Like its relatively near BET Group neighbours Ribble, Standerwick and North Western, BTC's Crosville of Chester was operating across the Mersey – northwards to Blackpool and southwards to the Midlands and London. Crosville spurned the pleasures of Midland Red's Digbeth coach station, just down the road a bit from the Bull Ring, and staged in suburban Erdington, more or less where Birmingham City Transport's last tram route, the No 2, had terminated until the trams were replaced in 1953. New-look ECW 39-seat bodywork adorns Bristol MW6G CMG429 (810 XFM), new that year, as it leaves the Erdington staging post en route from London to Liverpool (not via the motorway, service X2, which staged at the Swan Hotel, Lichfield – see next photograph) on service X1 on 24 June 1962.   *A. F. Porter*

Scottish Omnibuses – Central Scottish Motor Traction Company

Above:

Central SMT had a Glasgow to London service via Carlisle, Penrith, Boroughbridge, and the A1. This was not it, however. This, as Central's No B7 (WSF 207) clearly announces, was a Touring duty. No B7, looking new, was an AEC Reliance with Burlingham 34-seat bodywork which had been placed in service the previous year. It was photographed in the Swan Hotel yard, Lichfield, a place not too unfamiliar with the coaching trade, on 9 June 1962.   *A. F. Porter*

Southdown Motor Services

Below:

Like many other operators had for years, and as many of them still do, Southdown and its clients found that touring the Lakes, then Scotland, had an irresistible appeal. Here, southbound and heather-clad from some vast northern moor, Leyland Leopard L2 No 1724 (2724 CD), a 1961 coach with Harrington bodywork, climbs up the Parade in Sutton Coldfield on 26 August 1961.   *A. F. Porter*

Eastern Counties Omnibus Company

Above:
It has to be assumed that, labelled 'Private', ECOC's Bristol MW6G No LS815 (3815 PW) with the new-style bodywork, was indeed on private hire, but the place – Pool Meadow, Coventry – did get its ECOC summer Saturdays visitors, travelling between Birmingham and East Anglian resorts. No LS815 was new in 1962 and the photograph was taken on 13 August 1962. STL 707 was Delaine's No 53, a Bedford SB3 with Yeates Fiesta 41-seat coachwork, and was new in 1961. *A. F. Porter*

Eastern National Omnibus Company

Below:
Unquestionably on private hire duties, with nothing more formally-organised reaching any point within very many miles of Birmingham, Bristol MW6G No 486 – later No 338 – (285 NHK) of Braintree garage, with 39-seat old-style ECW bodywork, new in 1959, stands quietly in a corner of Midland Red's Sutton Coldfield garage on 23 June 1962. *A. F. Porter*

The Independent Operators and Miscellaneous Bus Users

Of the independent operators then – and now – the most pertinent observation is that they were their own masters, owing nothing to distant boards of parent companies, or commissions, or committees. Occasionally they entered into profitable joint service agreements with another operator and tasted the frustrations of a more remote control but, on the whole, they prospered or they fell by what they alone determined they should do.

Many of the country's present operators on the grand scale were not created large, but grew and grew, at times from strikingly modest origins. Their past was, just occasionally, flamboyantly independent, sometimes even roguishly so. Those independents of the Midlands which survived disaster, dissolution or acquisition by a national group were mostly small in scale, depending, usually, on essentially rural services in an area not squeezed until it popped by a major operator; they found a niche and occupied it, offering as well, often enough, the pleasures of a coaching run. Many still do. Not all were small concerns, however. By 1950 several independent operators had reached a most impressive scale and style of operation and in the Midlands one name stood out. It does so still – Barton Transport. The majority of those independent operators whose vehicles are represented here, however, were relatively small and typify the independent operator nationally as much as those with Midlands roots.

The use of valuable space for vehicles that were not in public service may seem wasteful, but even though they were not in public service those vehicles illustrated here had been so once and were buses still, or something very close. Whatever category they occupied they were part of the PSV scene and deserve some mention. If nothing more, the fairgrounds of the period without their showmen's buses would have been as conspicuously anachronistic as their counterparts a generation earlier without their Burrell and Fowler and Foster showmen's engines. Those buses played a part, long after they had run for Midland Red, or Trent, or Lincolnshire.

Barton Transport

Above:
Former City of Oxford Motor Services vehicles were always popular with other operators and this AEC Regent 0661, new in 1935 to Oxford as L71 (BFC 48), served Barton Transport as its No 665 for another eight years after being bought in 1951. It had Weymann 52-seat lowbridge bodywork. *Roy Marshall*

Below:
Several vehicles were bought from the West Riding Automobile Co in 1949/50, then also a major independent. Leyland Titan TD4 No 587 (HL 7432) with Roe bodywork was one of the oldest vehicles in the Barton fleet and had just been sold out of service when this photograph was taken at the vehicle auction complex at Measham, Leicestershire, on 12 August 1962. Barton's fleetnumber was still carried, although the fleetname had been obliterated. The other bus was former Atomic Energy Research Establishment Guy Arab GYL 419, once of London Transport. *A. F. Porter*

Above:

Notable amongst Barton's many ventures into the production of its own vehicles, utilising the chassis of some pre-existing vehicle and the company's ingenuity, was the BTS/1, based on the chassis of withdrawn prewar Leyland buses, often Lions, with Barton-built or commercial coachwork. Typical of these many vehicles was No 700 (OAL 815), constructed in the Barton workshops in 1953 from the remains of an ex-Bolton TD5 chassis once No 182, and a TD3c chassis section, once Preston's No 10, with Barton's own body. It was photographed at Mount Street bus station, Nottingham on 21 March 1962. *A. F. Porter*

Left:

At least as remarkable as the BTS/1 rebuilds were the double-deckers of the late 1950s based on Leyland PS1 and PS2 chassis which, though commercially bodied, produced ingeniously 'different' machines. No 822 (822 DNN) was created in 1959 from the chassis of DRV 155, a Leyland PS1 acquired from Doughty of King's Lynn as a single-deck coach, and carried Northern Counties lowbridge 63-seat bodywork. It was photographed travelling in Mount Street, Nottingham, on 2 April 1961. *A. F. Porter*

ROBIN
HOOD
I.P.A.
BARTON
DERBY
852
BARTON
852 FNN

BARTON
HOME
ALES
BARTON
BARTON
JVO 230
RN 8608
XG 9304

Left:

Also on the move in Mount Street, Nottingham, on 2 April 1961 was the rather more orthodox, though still stylishly bodied, No 852 (852 FNN), an AEC Regent V built in 1960 with Northern Counties 70-seat lowbridge bodywork, very similar to the 12ft 4½in Dennis Loline – the 'lowest of all time' 861 (861 HAL) – built in 1960 and also bodied by Northern Counties. *A. F. Porter*

Below left:

This line-up at Long Eaton Depot on 23 September 1962 is representative of Barton's early postwar mixed policy of buying new vehicles as and when it could and buying well-maintained second-hand vehicles from reliable sources, still pursued a decade later. It is rather remarkable, too, in that in one single, almost random, photograph three of the five vehicles appearing in it ultimately survived to be preserved in widely separated parts of the country and all of them far from Nottingham. From left to right the vehicles are: No 507 (JVO 230), one of 39 Leyland PD1s with Duple 55-seat lowbridge bodies delivered new to the company in 1947/48; No 918 (RN 8608), a 1939 Leyland TD5 with Alexander 53-seat lowbridge body built in 1950, formerly Ribble Motor Services No 2043 and acquired in 1961; No 844 (DJF 339), one of 16 ex-Leicester Leyland PD1s acquired in 1959/60. They were built with Leyland 56-seat bodies in 1946, and 844 had been No 238 in the Leicester City fleet. It is the vehicle featured under the Leicester heading, taken 13 years earlier; No 828 (XG 9304), a 1947 Leyland PD1 with Northern Counties 53-set lowbridge body, originally No 52 in the Middlesbrough Corporation fleet, acquired from Yuille of Larkhall in 1959; and No 440 (GNN 544), a 1945 Guy Arab II with Strachan 55-seat lowbridge body, one of 11 new to Barton.

Nos 507, 828, and 844 are those which are now preserved. *A. F. Porter*

Above:

One of the most visually striking vehicles to appear in the 1960s was the Bedford VAL14, a 36ft front-engined twin-steering three-axle vehicle, unveiled at the Commercial Motor Show in 1962. By the middle of 1963 two, Nos 970 and 971, were in the Barton fleet and by the end of 1964 20 were in service. No 994 (994 VRR), seen here in Nottingham in March 1968, carried Harrington 52-seat coachwork and was new in 1964. *G. H. F. Atkins*

Below:

The acquisition of Hall Bros (South Shields) Ltd by Barton Transport in July 1967, together with the Hall Brothers' North Shields subsidiary, Taylor Bros, added 35 coaches and the Newcastle upon Tyne to Coventry service to the Barton operation. Amongst the coaches included in the acquisition were no fewer than nine Bedford VAL14s, one of which, as Barton Transport No 1123 (CCU 276D), was photographed in Nottingham in June 1969. No 1123 had Duple 52-seat coachwork and had been acquired new by Hall Brothers in 1966. *G. H. F. Atkins*

Austin's of Stafford

Above:
Like many small independents this long-lived concern, (now called Happy Days (Woodseaves) Ltd), began most modestly when Mr W. H. Austin bought in 1927 the bus he drove for its Woodseaves owner. The vagaries of postwar transport gave the company – by then formally known as G. H. Austin & Son Ltd – considerable economic problems and led, after a period in receivership begun in 1969, to the reconstruction of the company in 1971 under its present name and one which, as a later illustration shows, perpetuates the name that G. H. Austin & Son used on its coaching fleet. Before 1963, however, the company had operated stage carriage as well as coaching and other activities, had expanded through the acquisition of other businesses, and had several garages in Staffordshire. Typical of small operators Austin's bought good second-hand vehicles when it could and was one of several independents which acquired former Ribble Motor Services 'White Ladies' when they became available, albeit no longer white but red, in 1960. The first Ribble 'White Ladies' went into service in 1949. They were coach-bodied Leyland PD1/3s, the 49-seat double-deck bodies being provided by Burlingham. On conversion to stage-carriage service – and red livery – the seating capacity was increased to 53. Nos 30 (BRN 273) and 41 (BRN 276), seen here at Lammascote Road, Stafford, on 11 March 1961, had previously been Nos 1213 and 1216 in the Ribble fleet.   *A. F. Porter*

Above right:
No 69 (URE 680) in the Austin fleet was this Bedford OB with Duple Vista body photographed on a day trip to Sutton Park, Sutton Coldfield, on 18 August 1962.   *A. F. Porter*

Right:
The trading name 'Happy Days' emblazoned on the panelling – and just visible behind the windscreen – anticipates by nine years the formal change of name the company was eventually to undergo. No 103 (VBF 2) was a Bedford SB5 with Duple 41-seat body new in 1962. It had joined No 69 on the day trip to Sutton Park on 18 August 1962.   *A. F. Porter*

PRIVATE

GNU 750

Blue Bus Services.

Blue Bus Services.

702 PRA

Tailby & George: Blue Bus Services, Willington, Derbyshire

Above left:

Prior to its acquisition by Derby Corporation in 1973 this well-known independent operator had for very many years provided stage-carriage and coach services from Willington, a village between Derby and Burton-on-Trent. For very many years it had depended almost exclusively on Daimler chassis but later bought two Dennis Lolines, both of which passed to Derby Corporation. Most of the surviving Blue Bus Services vehicles were destroyed by fire at Willington in 1976 but one which most fortuitously had passed into private ownership and preservation was this Daimler COG5 with Willowbrook 35-seat coachwork. It was built in 1939 and was photographed at Tailby & George's Willington premises on 29 August 1962.   *A. F. Porter*

Left:

Like those of many much larger opertors the Blue Bus stage-carriage services were frequently entrusted to the Daimler CVG6. In this picture, taken in Willington on 19 September 1962, CVG6 702 PRA, new in 1960 and carrying a Willowbrook 55-seat old-style lowbridge body, is on its way from Derby to Burton. 702 PRA was built with a batch for the South China Bus Company of Hong Kong. It was destroyed in the 1976 fire.   *A. F. Porter*

Brown's Blue, Markfield, Leicestershire

Above:

This independent was fairly typical of those moderately-sized concerns which owed their existence to a niche in the local coach market and a stage-carriage operation within a geographical area not fully exploited by a major operator. In this case the operator was Midland Red and in 1963 Brown's Blue was absorbed, following Kemp & Shaw of Leicester and Boyer of Rothley, near Loughborough, into Midland Red ownership. Unlike those acquisitions, however, none of the Brown's Blue buses entered Midland Red service. Like many such operators Brown's Blue had depended heavily on the second-hand purchase of larger operators' surplus vehicles and these were unlikely, by 1963, to have much impressed Midland Red's engineers. Typical of such vehicles in Brown's Blue fleet was KWB 85, an AEC Regent III with Northern Coachbuilders 56-seat body, new to Sheffield City Transport in 1947 as that undertaking's 'A' fleet No 585. It was bought by Brown's Blue in 1959 and was identical to No 6 (KWB 86) in the fleet of Stevenson's of Spath. Seen at Ibstock garage, 14 June 1962.   *A. F. Porter*

BAGWORTH
DJF 323

IBSTOCK
KOD 592

Above left:
Former Leicester City vehicles found many willing purchasers, Brown's Blue amongst them. DJF 323 had been No 228 in the Leicester City Transport fleet until its sale in July 1959. It was an AEC Regent II with Weymann 56-seat body, new to Leicester in 1946, and was photographed at Ibstock garage on 14 June 1962.   *A. F. Porter*

Left:
On a mellow August morning in 1962 – the last day of August, in fact – Brown's Blue AEC Regent III KOD 592 awaits developments outside Ibstock garage. It had been new to Devon General in 1949 as DR592 and had only recently been bought by the Markfield operator when the photograph was taken. Weymann 56-seat bodywork was fitted.   *A. F. Porter*

Butter's, Child's Ercall, near Market Drayton, Shropshire

Above:
H. Butter & Co operated a modest stage-carriage and coaching service from Child's Ercall, running into Market Drayton and the surrounding countryside; nowadays its coaches can be seen rather further afield. Local services were quite typical of those provided by the small independent rural concern, relying largely on second-hand vehicles. In this scene in Alexandra Road, Market Drayton, smartly-liveried AHE 776, a Leyland PS1 with Roe 32-seat body, new to Yorkshire Traction in 1947 as that company's No 754, pulls out to pass, presumably, the photographer's car. Butter's acquired AHE 776 in 1959; the photograph of it was taken on 3 July 1962.   *A. F. Porter*

26
URF 841
7
GKR 748
AUSTIN
992 GDH

RBB
DON EVERALL
DJ 9919
3
HKL 847

Churchbridge Luxury Coaches, Cannock, Staffordshire

Left:
This deceptively 'ordinary' line-up at Churchbridge's Cannock premises is of interest for more than just the presence of the Austin truck — which many overseas operators would have found irresistibly suitable for the attachment of passenger-carrying bodywork. The interest lies in Nos 7 and 26 in the Churchbridge fleet. No 7 (GKR 748) was a Bristol K5G new to Chatham & District Traction Company in 1942. In 1951 it received a new Weymann 56-seat body and in 1955 became DH440 in the Maidstone & District fleet, which had absorbed Chatham & District. It was delicensed by the end of 1960, after which it joined other ex-M&D vehicles in the Churchbridge fleet. Several former Maidstone & District vehicles were to see Midlands service, though few had served Chatham & District.

No 26 (URF 841) was interesting for quite different reasons. Firstly, it was a Maudslay — chassis No 79518 — and secondly it carried rare coachwork by Metalcraft, a Staffordshire coachbuilder which had manufactured only some 50 or 60 bodies when construction ceased in the late 1950s. It was one of a pair with 37-seat coachwork built for Churchbridge in 1951 and was photographed on 4 August 1962.   *A. F. Porter*

Below left:
Another former Maidstone & District Bristol in Churchbridge ownership was K6A No 3 (HKL 847), new to M&D in 1947 with Weymann 56-seat bodywork as its No DH164. Though five years younger than DH440 it was released from Maidstone service more quickly and was acquired by Churchbridge in 1959. The other vehicle in this picture, taken on 24 June 1961 in Sutton Park, Sutton Coldfield, where many day trip buses could be seen in the summer months, was Don Everall's (of Wolverhampton) DJ 9919, a Leyland PD1 with East Lancashire 55-seat body, formerly St Helen's Corporation No 43, new in 1947 and acquired by the Wolverhampton operator not long before the photograph was taken. The vehicle behind DJ 9919 was JP 5526, an all-Leyland 55-seat PD1, formerly No 144 in the Wigan Corporation fleet and also in Don Everall ownership.   *A. F. Porter*

Corvedale Motors, Ludlow, Shropshire

Below:
No longer wholly independent but part of the otherwise independent Whittle Group of Highley, in the Severn Valley, the Corvedale Motor Co was once a very active independent operator in Ludlow and the surrounding countryside although it had its origins in a concern founded in 1930 in Pontrilas, south-west of Hereford on the Monmouth border. The Whittle Group acquired Corvedale Motors in 1969 and has, by a marked preference for Bedford chassis, perpetuated the choice of an earlier generation of Bedford users, typified by this Corvedale Motors Bedford SBO No 23 (RTX 497). It had a Nudd Brothers 40-seat body and had been acquired by Corvedale from Williams of Treorchy in 1959. The photograph, despite the unambiguous Ludlow destination, was taken well off Corvedale's normal routes, on 22 May 1961 in the Parade, Sutton Coldfield, whilst on hire to Don Everall.   *A. F. Porter*

W. Gash & Sons, Newark

Right:
Many rural operators began in the most modest way imaginable, often providing a transport service as an activity ancillary to their main business. Many vanished from our roads long ago though a few, like W. Gash & Sons Ltd of Newark, whose enterprise began in 1919, are with us still. It has a fleet of two dozen or so buses and coaches, and is involved in stage-carriage as well as coach work. In this July 1951 view Strachan-bodied Daimler CVD6 DD3 (KAL 580), new in 1948, running on the Nottingham route that had long been the mainstay of the stage-carriage services operated by the firm, waits for passengers. DD3 was rebodied in 1958 and is privately preserved though sister DD1 (KAL 578) is remarkably still in **service.** *G. H. F. Atkins*

Green Bus Company, Rugeley, Staffordshire

Bottom left:

Like Brown's Blue of Markfield and the nearby Harper Brothers operation at Heath Hayes the Green Bus Co provided services in an area not adequately served by any major operator but, with Harpers, was eventually acquired by Midland Red. Prior to its acquisition by the Birmingham & Midland empire in 1973 the Green Bus Co had been an interesting independent operator providing a full range of services with a very mixed, substantially second-hand, fleet. Some of its more modern vehicles, indeed, were sufficiently up-to-date and sound to be placed in service in the Midland Red fleet, though not for very long. In the late 1950s and early 1960s the Green Bus fleet had not attained that degree of sophistication. Its vehicles had frequently seen several years of service with a major undertaking – Northern General Transport, Ribble, Bradford, Liverpool, Sheffield and Southampton Corporations, for example – before receiving the two shades of green of Green Bus. In this scene former Bradford City Transport No 552 (EKY 552), by then No 38 in the Green Bus fleet, gets hosed down in the Rugeley garage yard on 16 September 1962. No 38 was a Daimler CVD6 with Brush 56-seat bodywork new to Bradford in 1948. It had been acquired by the Green Bus Company in 1959.   *A. F. Porter*

Right:

The Foden PVD6 chassis was not produced in large numbers and was thus something of a rarity. The combination of Foden chassis and Samlesbury bodywork was distinctly unusual but the Green Bus Co had two such vehicles, No 26 (SRE 881) and No 28 (TRF 601), seen in this photograph waiting to leave Rugeley for Cannock on 17 July 1960. They were built in 1949 and 1950 respectively and seated 53 passengers. Neither of them survived for preservation.   *A. F. Porter*

Below:

A more common vehicle placed in service in 1947 was No 35 (NRE 543), a Guy Arab II with Northern Coachbuilders 55-seat body. It was photographed in Eastgate Street, Stafford, on 11 March 1961 on the route to Uttoxeter, where the company had an outstation garage. A notable feature of the Green Bus Co's operation was its routes to places served by Midland Red, PMT and Trent, as well as penetration to the heartland of the Stevenson operation. For a small concern it held its ground remarkably well.   *A. F. Porter*

Harper Brothers, Heath Hayes, Cannock, Staffordshire

Above:

The pale green buses and coaches of the company known formally as Harper Brothers (Heath Hayes) Ltd were a very familiar sight in South Staffordshire for very many years prior to the company's acquisition by Midland Red in 1974. With the licensing of its route to Birmingham Harper Brothers reached the heart of the West Midlands conurbation and with many of its vehicles going into service with Midland Red after the 1974 acquisition they were to continue to be seen there for several years more. In the late 1950s and the early 1960s, however, when its bus operations were rather more localised and the acquisition of a modern fleet was still a future event, the company had a typical independent operator's somewhat mixed fleet, substantially second-hand, of around 40 vehicles. Some acquisitions proved a sound investment, including ex-London Transport RTs and identical buses from St Helen's Corporation, plus newly-built coaches – including the last four Guy Arab LUFs to be built – but many others were no more than the expediency purchases of an operator struggling to survive against falling revenues and increasing overheads. This RT-type AEC Regent III was one of those from St Helen's, new in 1952 as No D8. No 10 (BDJ 808) in the Harper fleet had Park Royal 56-seat bodywork and was bought from St Helen's early in 1962. The photograph was taken at Heath Hayes garage on 6 April 1962. The bus itself has since been preserved.   *A. F. Porter*

Below:

Far from home and looking just a little mournful Harper No 57 (1291 RE) stands waiting for a call to duty in a coach park at Paignton, Devon, on 21 May 1960. No 57, one of the last four Guy Arab LUFs, was new in 1959 and carried Willowbrook Viking 41-seat coachwork.   *A. F. Porter*

Above:

The less glamorous, though infinitely pleasing side of independent operation on the shoestring scale, is typified, perhaps, by this illustration, typical very much of Harper's fleet of the period and typical, too, of the industry's smaller private operators everywhere at that time. Three vehicles stand quietly outside the Heath Hayes premises on 4 August 1962. They are, from the left: No 40 (SRE 146), a 1949 Crossley SD42 with Burlingham 35-seat bus body, new to Harper's; No 18 (KUE 373), a 1951 Dennis Lancet with Yeates 39-seat coachwork, new to Hastilow's of Sutton Coldfield; No 53 (JDK 80), an almost identical 1951 vehicle acquired with the Dunn & Hale business of Brownhills.

Ten years later the Harper Brothers image was one of modernity with PD3As, Fleetlines, and Leyland Leopards. It was to be a short-lived success story. *A. F. Porter*

J. Lloyd & Son, Nuneaton, Warwickshire

Below:

Still going strong in the works contract and coach business, almost exclusively using Bedfords, Lloyds of Nuneaton has, nevertheless, occasionally operated distinctly unusual vehicles during its 60-year history. One most distinctive acquisition was STF 90, the prototype Leyland PDR1 Lowloader. STF 90 was bought from Scottish Motor Traction in 1958 when that concern acquired Lowland Motorways. It had been built in 1953, bodied by Saunders-Roe, and, with a second similar vehicle, led to the PDR1/1 Atlantean of 1956. *Robert Mack collection*

Mid-Wales Motorways, Newtown, Montgomeryshire

Above:

Representing not an absorption of Montgomeryshire – or the present Powys – into the Midlands but only a Mid-Wales Motorways route into Shrewsbury is this picture taken in Hill's Lane parking area, Shrewsbury, on 7 August 1962. Ex-Corvedale Motors Sentinel STC4/Beadle GUX 524 with 40-seat bodywork stands alongside FFM 273, a former Crosville Guy Arab II with Northern Counties 53-seat body.   *A. F. Porter*

F. Procter & Son, Hanley, Stoke-on-Trent

Below:

Many independents in the Potteries succumbed to Potteries Motor Traction competition and were acquired but a few, including F. Procter & Son Ltd, survived and are still in operation. Procter's has never been a large undertaking but it has had a continuous existence since 1922. Quite typical of the surviving Potteries independent fleets of the period is Procter's GBW 336, a 1953 Daimler CVD6 with Massey bodywork. It was acquired by Procter's from Ronsway of Hemel Hempstead in 1958 and was photographed in Leek Road, Bucknall, on 5 October 1962.   *A. F. Porter*

Salopia Saloon Coaches, Whitchurch, Shropshire

Above:

This well-known North Shropshire independent is now, after a few years in the ownership of Gold Case Travel of Middlesbrough and thence of the Ellerman Group, owned by Shearing's of Altrincham. It originated in 1926 in Whitchurch and was wholly independent for many years, providing bus services in the Whitchurch area but depending mainly on its coaching activities. Typical of its local services — and typical, indeed, of many smaller Shropshire undertakings of the 1950s — was this Bedford OB, No 81 (GNT 316) on the Whitchurch to Market Drayton service. No 81 was built in 1950 and had Mulliner 31-seat bodywork. It was photographed in Market Drayton on 30 April 1960.   *A. F. Porter*

South Notts Bus Company, Gotham, Nottinghamshire

Right:

Curiously, it might seem, this independent operator whose services from Gotham began in 1928 has remained quite free from Barton influence, despite Barton's having had a half share in the business for many years. Nothing of the connection was or is visually apparent in the quite separate fleets of the two closely connected companies.

No 1 (RR 3116) in the South Notts fleet lasted for many years after its working life was over but did not, unfortunately, last long enough to be preserved. It was a Guy BA with 20-seat Guy body, new in 1926. Not quite beyond recognition, it was photographed at the Gotham garage on 23 September 1962.   *A. F. Porter*

Above:

Somewhat unusually for an independent operator – and especially so for one so closely associated with Barton – South Notts has always had stage services as its main activity and double-decker buses have long outnumbered coaches in its fleet. New to South Notts in 1954 was No 55 (RRR 912), a Leyland PD2/20 with Weymann lowbridge 55-seat bodywork. It was photographed in The Rushes, Loughborough, on 22 August 1962, en route to Nottingham.   *A. F. Porter*

Below:

One direction in which South Notts did resemble its Barton partners was in the occasionally purchase of reliable second-hand vehicles from well-maintained fleets. No 77 (CCK 663) was one of a few vehicles acquired from Ribble in 1961. It was a Leyland PD2/3 with Brush lowbridge 53-seat bodywork and had been new to Ribble in 1949. No 77, which had been No 2687 in the Ribble fleet and has now been preserved, was photographed on the South Notts Gotham premises on 26 June, 1962. Another former Ribble vehicle stands behind it.   *A. F. Porter*

Stevenson's, Spath, Uttoxeter, Staffordshire

Above:

Now rather formally known as Stevenson's of Uttoxeter Ltd this distinctly vigorous operator, quite unafraid of PMT breathing down its neck, or of Trent or Midland Red's less immediately threatening presence, was established in the not altogether obvious village of Spath in 1926. It has grown today to the point at which it has seen expansion and modernisation allow it to acquire a number of former PMT and Midland Red routes. Much of the modernisation has been by the purchase of second-hand vehicles but the fleet today is, even so, very different in character from the one that operated from Spath 25 years ago. Then, although it had been in existence for more than 30 years, the Company was still somewhat tentatively pushing its services out into East Staffordshire with a rather elderly and mainly second-hand fleet. But it was confident and advertised itself rather than the products of others on its striking yellow- and black-liveried buses; its services were varied, too, as the self-help advertisements in these illustrations show. In this picture No 6 (KWB 86), formerly 586 in the Sheffield City Transport 'A' fleet (identical to KWB 85 in Brown's Blue fleet) stands in Wetmore Road bus station, Burton-on-Trent, on 11 September 1961. No 6 was an AEC Regent III with Northern Coachbuilders 56-seat body. It was new in 1947 and acquired in 1959.   *A. F. Porter*

Below:

Five years older than No 6 and essentially a prewar vehicle No 19 in the Stevenson fleet, though bearing no more than its registration number, FON 326 makes its way along Horninglow Street en route to Ashbourne on 11 September 1961. It was an all-Leyland TD7 new to Birmingham City Transport in 1942 as No 1326. It was one of the very few wartime buses placed in service in Birmingham with non-utility bodywork, was withdrawn in 1954 and sold to Stevenson's, but, unlike 1330, also sold to Stevenson's, did not survive to be preserved.   *A. F. Porter*

Above:

Many operators took advantage of the availability of former London Transport RTs when they were placed on the market, Stevenson's amongst them. Stevenson's also bought this ex-London Transport Leyland Titan PD2/1 (7RT) 1949 RTL with Park Royal bodywork, formerly RTL270. It was acquired in 1960 and was photographed in Uttoxeter as Stevenson's No 29 (KGU 216) on 28 March 1960. The other vehicle in the picture, No 21 (FA 8532) was a Guy Arab III with Guy bodywork and had been No 1 in the Burton Corporation fleet before its acquisition by Stevenson's.

Vigo Coachways, Brownhills, Staffordshire

Below:

Les Owen's Vigo Coachways was not a major independent but was a concern which, like many similar coach operations, came to possess very interesting buses from time to time, long after they had left their original owners. FXT 315, in dazzling livery, had been new to the London Passenger Transport Board in 1940 and was acquired by Les Owen from Smith of March in 1960. It was an AEC Regent (2RT2) with LPTB body and had been RT140. It was photographed at the firm's Brownhills premises on 7 April 1960. *A. F. Porter*

Fleet Car Sales, Dunchurch, Warwickshire

Above:
Second-hand vehicles do not always pass from operator to operator direct; many pass via dealers. One Midland dealer was this firm which, on the day that this photograph was taken, 21 April 1960, had vehicles in stock that had been sold by United Automobile Services, Sunderland Corporation, Durham District Services, West Yorkshire, Yorkshire Woollen District, City of Oxford Motor Services, South Wales Transport and Western National, amongst others. This picture is of HHN 965, an ex-Durham District Guy Arab. *A. F. Porter*

Bird's, Stratford-upon-Avon

Left:
Bird's was a place where some vehicles found new owners but where many met their ends. Being manoeuvred into position in the breaking area is former Birmingham City Transport No 1052 (CVP 152), a 1937 Daimler COG5 with Metro-Cammell 54-seat body, one of a bulk purchase of prewar and early postwar vehicles made by Bird's when Birmingham cleared its fleet of older vehicles in 1960 and 1961. The photograph was taken on 15 April 1961. *A. F. Porter*

Left:

Another former Birmingham vehicle at Bird's premises on 15 April 1961, though not transferred down to the breaking area, was No 814 (BOP 814), a 1936 Daimler COG5. No 814 was one of a few vehicles which was badly damaged during the blitz. Its own BRCW body was repaired and transferred to No 901 in 1941 and in 1942 814 received the English Electric body seen here, originally built for fitting on new Daimler chassis for Manchester City Transport that were destroyed in the Coventry factory in the blitz. Birmingham had 20 of these Manchester bodies.   *A. F. Porter*

Henry Boot

Below:

This firm is one of the many contractors which have acquired second-hand vehicles for the transport of their own workforce. The somewhat battered vehicle seen here in Walsall on 7 April 1960, had been the once pristine Trent 706 (RC 4607), shown under that heading.   *A. F. Porter*

Roberts Brothers Circus

Right:

Many former SOS vehicles of the Midland Red, Trent, and Potteries fleets found their way into showmen's hands. This SOS 'SON' was new in 1939 to Trent, as that company's No 402 (RC 7091). It had Willowbrook 34-seat bodywork and was photographed at Robert Brothers circus site in Willenhall, Staffordshire, on 19 April 1960.   *A. F. Porter*

Wednesbury Corporation

Below right:

Whilst several Midland Red SOSs ended their lives on staff transport or for showland use, Wednesbury Corporation modified SOS 'SON' 1935 (CHA 559) as a mobile library after it was withdrawn by BMMO in 1958. It had English Electric 39-seat bodywork when new in 1936 and this had been revitalised by Nudd Brothers and Lockyer in 1950 or thereabouts. It was photographed in operation in Wednesbury on 11 May 1960.   *A. F. Porter*

RC 7091
BOROUGH of WEDNESBURY
MOBILE LIBRARY
CHA 559

Sutton Coldfield Old People's Welfare Committee

Above:
The use of buses for social welfare purposes, both officially and voluntarily organised, has increased in recent years but few such bodies will have utilised a vehicle so decidedly uncommon as a former London Passenger Transport Board AEC Q. The Sutton Coldfield Committee did precisely that with ex-London Transport Q83 (CGJ 188), built in 1935 with a BRCW 35-seat body. It was photographed in Sutton Coldfield Midland Red garage, where it rested whilst not in use, on 6 May 1961. Fortunately, Q83 is one of the species to have been preserved.   *A. F. Porter*

British Railways

Below:
Many years after the last of the railway companies disposed of its own public bus services British Railways continued to use buses for its own operational purposes – although, of course, it still hires vehicles when engineering works prevent the operation of advertised trains, or occasionally operates timetable services entirely by bus in conjunction with a major operator. The use of buses in British Railways ownership was, however, limited solely to its own needs and second-hand vehicles were bought as required. In this picture Midland Region No 851-SO M (HKL 842) stands in Long Street, Walsall, on 21 August 1961. It was an AEC Regal with Beadle 36-seat bodywork, new in 1946 as No SO 32 in the Maidstone & District fleet.   *A. F. Porter*

0   10   20   30   40 Miles
LIVERPOOL BAY
YORKSHIRE
East Riding
West Riding
LANCASHIRE
Humber
Mersey
Dee
FLINT
CHESHIRE
Whitchurch
Market Drayton
Chesterfield
NOTTS
Lincoln
LINCOLN
Newark
Nottingham
DERBY
Stoke on Trent
STAFFORD
Derby
Willington
Uttoxeter
Stafford
Burton upon Trent
Rugeley
Shrewsbury
Cannock
Wolverhampton
Markfield
LEICESTER
Leicester
RUTLAND
Walsall
West Bromwich
Nuneaton
Ludlow
Birmingham
Coventry
SHROPSHIRE
WORCESTER
WARWICK
NORTHAMPTON
HUNTINGDON